PANDORA'S BOX OF 101 SINS

A Book Based on the Holy Bible

Christian Heritage Rediscovered

The Series, as the name suggests, is meant to focus on Christian Faith & Living vis-à-vis topics like Literature & Poetry, Indigenous Philosophizing, Ethical response towards Agriculture, Health & Healing, Science & Technology, Ecofeminist Theology, Sociological approach towards Human Rights, Law & Politics, Arts, History of Ideas, Ancient Civilizations, Cultural Contiguity, Religious Cosmologies & Mysticism, Footsteps of famous Theologians, World Peace & Harmony, Global Capitalism, Network Marketing, Cybertheology, Population & Demographics, Epigraphic Studies, Contextualized Education, and many others. We welcome a Mss. on any topic/s mentioned, whether they are original works, scholarly monographs, collections of conference papers, revised dissertations, or translations of historical documents. Through the Series we, the Publishers, are striving to put forward published works that may help Institutions, Academic Bodies, Researchers, Scholars and the World at large in furthering their respective knowledge and understanding on the concerned subject. We welcome your comments on our efforts and further suggestions on how we can foster the upcoming thoughtful theologically grounded books.

Christian Heritage Rediscovered - 9

PANDORA'S BOX OF 101 SINS

A Book Based on the Holy Bible

Dr. Lovely

CWI

Christian World Imprints™

First Published in 2014 by

Christian World Imprints(TM)
Christian Publishing & Books from India
H-12 Bali Nagar, **New Delhi-110015**
info@christianworldimprints.com
www.ChristianWorldImprints.com
Phone: +91 11 25465925 Fax: +91 11 25173055

ISBN-13: 978-93-5148-017-4 ISBN-10: 93-5148-017-8

Cataloging in Publication Data--DK
Courtesy: D.K. Agencies (P) Ltd. <docinfo@dkagencies.com>

Lovely, 1970-
Pandora's box of 101 sins : a book based on the Holy Bible / Lovely.
p. cm. -- (Christian heritage rediscovered ; 9)
ISBN 9789351480174
ISBN 9351480178

1. Sin--Biblical teaching. 2. Christian life--Biblical teaching. 3. Bible--Criticism, interpretation, etc. I. Title. II. Title: Pandora's box of one hundred one sins. III. Series: Christian heritage rediscovered ; 9.

DDC 241.3 23

Printed at Chawla Offset Printers

Dedicated to

My almighty God for all the blessings, love and support

My dear husband **Dr. Biji Thomas George**

My loving son **Joshua George Thomas**

My loving father **Dr. J. M. Sebastian**

My affectionate brother **Mr. Leslie M. Joseph**

My ever supporting mother-in law
Mrs. Shanthamma George

I specially remember my prayer warrior father-in-law
Late Mr. P. T. George
&
My affectionate and caring mother
Late Mrs. Mary M.

The Book

The Book brings out the quest of Author in finding out the answers of several questions that used to trouble her. Questions like: Why her prayers are not answered? Why she feels burdened in heart? Why is she stagnant in her Christian life? Why is she suffering from fear, anxiety, and lack of confidence? These notes are the answers, the truths, that she encountered in the Holy Bible. The truths reveal the words of God in terms of: How does God consider the issue of Sins? Is there a dichotomy between the Old and the New Testaments on the subject of Sins? Can a child of God afford to sit on the fence on the issue of Sins?

This Book includes the commonest Sins that are categorized under - **Sins Against God**, **Sins Against Others**, and **Sins Against Self**; and finally paves the way for the readers to be **A Good Christian**. It is meant for those who are willing to gauge the spiritual meter of their faith; who are ready to assess themselves concerning the words of God; who accepts their Sins and are geared up for repercussion.

Finally, the Author believes that the Holy Spirit will intercede with each person who employs these notes in their day to day life. Understanding these **Sins** and their consequences can liberate the readers from the bondage of **Sins** and can lead them closer to God.

The Author

Dr. Lovely is an Eminent Dentist, both practicing and teaching dentistry in Trivandrum, India. She has authored several books in the field of Dentistry. Originally, from a Catholic/Syrian Jacobite family, she was born-again when in Dental School. As the first born-again person in her extended family she faced many difficulties in reading and understanding the Holy Bible as there was no one to guide or teach her.

Therefore, she had to spend many hours in reading the Holy Bible to grow in her Christian life. By God's grace this study helped her in motivating and guiding many others who are looking for answers from the Holy Book.

Foreword

The Value of Truth

In life, value determines the worth of anything or any endeavour. To attach value to someone, an object, situation or even a matter implies the worth or esteem placed on it, and this varies depending on different parameters for judgment or consideration at any given time. However, value is intrinsic and subjective; in other words, what is of value to an individual may virtually be worthless to another individual. This again explains why human beings differ from one place to the other on matters like money and possessions, religions and faith, politics and governance and other issues like marriage and divorce, beauty and love, and all such other considerations common to a man. Life has been so ordered to emphasize that value determines judgement, i.e., your assessment and decisions on critical and non-essential matters are very much based on your value systems. You tend to place value on issues like sustenance, faith, health, relationships, divinity, etc., that are critical to your existence as a person not only on the physical, material plane, but even more so on the spiritual and esoteric levels.

In the same way, people hold different opinions concerning the subject matter truth. There has never been a universally accepted definition of truth, whether as a concept or a philosophy. Our exercise here is not to try to define what truth is or is not. Rather we attempt to ascertain and build on a well-known point: truth is constant, it is revealing. From a Christian's point of view, seeking after the truth is a lifelong enterprise that determines the ultimate purpose in life. For a child of God, truth is beyond revealing the fact in any given situation; it is a living for that fact, a pursuit that defies limitation.

The pursuit of Jesus is the pursuit of truth because Jesus is the Truth.

"Thomas said unto him, Lord, we know not whither thou goest; and how can we know the way? Jesus saith unto him, I am the way THE TRUTH, and the life: no man cometh unto the Father, but by me."

As if to further reiterate the same issue, Jesus said unto "those who believed on him, if ye continue in my word, then are ye my disciples indeed: And ye shall know the truth, and the truth shall make you free". (Jn. 8:31-32)

The words of God open up the way for an understanding of the truth, sheds light on how to treat the truth and helps the child of God live his life in relation to the truth.

This book by Dr. Lovely "Pandora's Box of 101 Sins" takes you on a journey to discover the truth. You should only embark on this trip if you are ready to come to terms with the absolute truth as contained in the Bible, the infallible word of God. Therefore, if you are not ready for an encounter with the truth; if you are not willing to come to terms with the reality of what the truth is, then this book is not for you. The truth manifests; it reveals; and so from the pages of this book certain facts about the word of God leap out clean and clear. How does God consider the issue of Sins? Is there a dichotomy between the Old and the New Testament on the subject matter of Sins? Can a child of God afford to sit on the fence on the issue of Sins? The book contains questions to which the reader must be ready to proffer answers!

If you are willing to gauge the spiritual meter of your faith; if you are ready to assess yourself concerning the truth of the word of God; if you are willing to come to terms with your real estate on the issue of sin and its repercussions and if your relationship with your Maker and Creator takes precedence in your life beyond other primordial considerations, then you must painstakingly read through the pages of this book. The only guarantee I have for you is that this book will change you, and that, for the better!

For a believer in Christ Jesus, the standard gauge or meter of assessment or truth in any given human circumstances is the Bible. This book is an expose on God's unchanging attitude to sin whether in the old or new covenants. The Bible says that God is angry with the sinner every day. The author Dr. Lovely reminds us again that God hates Sins through and through and therefore urges His children pursue an uncompromising attitude towards them.

As I read through the manuscript, (I did this two or more times), I was tempted to be critical at some points of what the author describes as everlasting commandments of God, and other issues such as the teachings on the Sabbath day. I rationalized that the flaws in the laws of Moses had been corrected in the New Testament particularly in the light of the perfected works of atonement and redemption by the Lord of Jesus. True indeed! But the Holy Spirit immediately reminded me that oftentimes believers try to excuse away our attempts at compromising the severity of the word of God with such manner of thinking. I therefore charge you reader to drop any preconceived bias and study this book with the simplicity of your heart, approaching it as you would any direct instruction from God that leads to the unveiling of the truth. Remember that the value of truth is in its appreciation.

Let me commend this priceless material to you with this charge from the book of Proverbs:

Buy the truth and do not sell it. Pro. 23:23.

Olukayode O Owojori
Ibadan, Nigeria, 2012

Mr. Owojori is a Nigerian Christian Author and Human Capital Development Expert based in Ibadan, Headquarters of the South West region of the country. He is also a well-acclaimed Christian Drama Minister who has featured in several movies. He is currently doing research work on his Doctoral thesis in Peace and Conflict Studies.

Acknowledgements

I thank almighty God who enabled me to know Him and made me His child. I am greatly indebted to my husband Dr. Biji Thomas George without whose support, love and encouragement I could not have completed this book. This book could not have been a reality if God had not given me a husband who is loving, kind, encouraging and a perfectionist. My heartfelt thanks to my son Joshua George Thomas for his cooperation and patience. I thank my dear parents Dr. J. M. Sebastian and Mrs. Mary M. for their encouragement and support. I thank my dear brother Mr. Leslie M. Joseph for his never ending support. I thank God for all the people that I came across in this life from whom I could imbibe the good qualities and improve myself from their constructive criticisms. God provided me with wonderful in-laws, my father in law Late Mr. P. T. George and my mother in law Mrs. Shanthamma George and my husband's dear grandmother Mrs. Alleyamma Koshy, Ernakulum who guided, helped and supported me always. I fondly remember my sister in laws and their husbands, Mr. James Varghese and Mrs. Gibi James, Mr. Bijo Thomas and Dr. Liji Alice Thomas, Evangelist Koshy K. Paul and Mrs. Jili Grace George for their support and spiritual love. At this moment, I owe a big thanks to my husband's uncles and aunties and to specially mention Mr. K.V. John and Mrs. Elizabeth John, Thiruvalla and Adv Raju M. Koshy and family, Ernakulum. Apart from my immediate family I have admired many spiritual souls who guided me to grow spiritually. My thanks to Sister Sundaram, Sister Mercy, Sister Ruby, Brother Sam Daniel of Christ Church, Salem and Coimbatore. With immense gratitude, I remember my other spiritual mentors on my onward journey, Pastor Valsalan and family of Sulliya assembly,

Pastor Mathew Koshy and family of Anchal assembly; Pastor John Joseph and family of World Impact Church, Pastor Suresh, Pastor Biji and Dr. Nalini of Pilgrims Highland Church, Brother George. Kutty CYF, Mr. Alexander Jacob and Mrs. Elizabeth Alexander my prayer partners and finally my dear brothers and sisters in Brethren assembly, Pongamoodu. During my growth, born again as a Christian, many people outside the Christian community and within have influenced my thinking. I remember, Mr. V. Hamza, a dear family friend of ours for his dynamic capabilities. He is presently the organizer and owner of RICH Organization. I remember the ever helping cousin Mr. Thomas Mammen and Mrs. Anamika Mammen running the Grama Jyothi Institute for the mentally challenged at Trivandrum. I owe a lot to my dear Professor Dr. K. Chandrasekharan Nair for disciplining me and guiding me in my academic carrier. I learned a lot from the life of Dr. Beena Sam and Mr. Sam Mathews Thiruvalla, my good spiritual friends. I specially remember my dear friends Dr. Gayathri Sundari, Dr. Sreeja Carunacaran, Dr. Shyam Dev Vyasan and Dr. Vineetha Shyam, Mrs. Anandhi Shivakumar Chennai and my clinic assistant Sister Sheela. I remember with great joy my college days prayer partners Dr. Jessy John of Pushpagiri Medical College, Thiruvalla and Dr. Shylaja Thomas residing in U.K.

I am blessed to have young spiritual friends as Mrs. Jasmine Abbey in Trivandrum and Mrs. Praisy Byju in Muscat, Mr. Rejoy Sam and Mrs. Julie Rejoy in Kuwait. Many people I met along my journey had a great impact on my spiritual life, I vividly remember the ever smiling Ms. May from Malaysia presently residing in Tokyo and the Brothers at Ochanamizoo Brethren Assembly Tokyo, Brother David and Brother Steve, Brother John Nuletti and family, Sister Yedid M. and Brother Joel from U.S.A.

I am highly indebted to the Pongamoodu Brethren Assembly for their active role in my life. I fondly remember the dynamic youth group led by Brother Ebenezer, Brother Abbey and Brother Benjamin, an asset to this assembly to which I was a part for more than 13 long years till my husband moved to Oman. I remember the Seeb Brethren Assembly with gratitude and all who knowingly and unknowingly touched my life and made me what I am today, thank you very much.

I thank all the editors who painstakingly went through the contents and gave constructive suggestions on the book. I thank Asst. Editor Mrs. Rose Mary Phillip Thrissur, followed by Mr. Alexander Jacob, Principal of Vale College and Director of Studies in the Vale Tutorial College and his wife Elizabeth Alexander, Councilor and Food and Nutrition teacher at Vale College in Nigeria. Both of them are basically missionaries. I extend my thanks to Mr. Kayode Owojori an Author and Development Sector Expert and a good Christian who is involved in acting in TV Christian productions, Nigeria; who took time and effort to edit the title. I owe all my thanks to Pastor John Joseph, World Impact Community Church, Trivandrum who was the first person to read the entire manuscript and gave me constructive ideas on how to start the book. I thank him for his promptness and expert advice. I am especially indebted to Mr. Olukayode O Owojori, Nigerian Christian Author and Human Capital Development Expert based in Ibadan, Headquarters of the South West region of the country who has written the foreword of this book. I am thankful to him for taking time out of his busy schedule to go through the entire manuscript. And I am greatly indebted to Darya Crockett of Innovo Publishing, LLC for the free critique editing and constructive suggestions. At this point I remember Brian Grove at My Perfect Pitch (brianlgrove@live.co.uk), for his valuable advice and the website.

I thank Mr. Sudheer who was kind enough to design a cover page for this title. I thank my son Joshua for the cover page idea. Finally, I owe it all to the Christian World Imprints, Editors and Publishers.

Preface

This life is a precious time borrowed from God to prove our faithfulness towards Him. What more purpose can this life hold? We are pilgrims in this place and God through many of His prophets has revealed how man is to live in this world and has set standards of purity. Yet sometimes in certain situations God Himself permits a deviation to His plan for a special purpose. Now, as a committed Christian our main goal in this life should be to what extent we can testify God in our lives and glorify Him with our body. Enoch pleased God so much so that he never tasted death and so did Elijah. In short, the whole duty of a man is to fear God and to keep His commandments (Eccl: 11:13). If you love a person with your whole heart and soul you would not hurt that person by any means. After marriage if the decisions that partners make in their life are not in unison, the marriage life can fail; the same applies in each of our lives in regard to God, as our soul is inseparable from God. The commandments set forth by God are life-giving to the soul which in turn makes us happy and contended. The ultimate aim of every true Christian is eternal life. To abide by the commandments faithfully you need Christ to live within you. Christ within you will bring about the great changes in your life which you cannot achieve with your own ability or self will. I introspected into my past life and did an inspection on what I have achieved and how I am changed over the years. I realized that my perceptions of many matters have changed and how the consequences of bad decisions led to deleterious effects. I was also by now more equipped spiritually to view any situation lightly and to rest on God the burden to solve all the problems. The main reason for this change was the greatest decision of my life to accept Jesus as my saviour and be baptized. The origin of a change in man is definitely from his thought process. A man who thinks of how he can change for the good of a society and how he can help the less fortunates are the easiest category to involve in the process of change. To change into a new person overnight with goodness in words and deeds is a difficult process if tried with human wisdom. Contrary, if you take help from God, wishing sincerely and earnestly to be a good person and submitting all your weaknesses into His hands the task to be a good person becomes a menial job. Spiritual realm begins when a person starts to acknowledge the presence of God in his life. During this walk with God you tend to realize that unless God is given a place in your heart, your mind and body cannot be controlled of thoughts, actions or words. Down the memory lane of my life as a Christian, I learned that I went through many phases of Christian thoughts. The thought to know God more and more can only arise from a thoughtful mind, a mind that can see beyond the materialistic worldly ways.

During the initial phases, when you hear about the true God you need a mind to accept and believe it without questioning. Unless, God gives you that heart to accept the Holy Gospel, no man can receive it. Once accepted, you need to confess all your Sins with a repentant heart, acknowledging God alone will not change you into a new person. I was a person who till then believed that all Gods are the same and every religious practice leads to this one God. One fine day, the concept of only one living God who is no idol was conveyed to me. This concept was totally new to my existing belief and a statement that I always argued about with a stubborn mind. But one day, the same concept of one God was conveyed to me by a person who I admired a lot for his righteous ways and goodness he possessed in his life. When a statement is made by a person with good testimony then it stirs your heart, you get sleepless nights and slowly I also started to enquire within myself, Am I really happy? Am I courageous to face any situations in my life? Can I really depend on the belief system that I presently follow? Confusion occurred within me and this kept me pondering for months to understand which is the right path to eternal life when I was just 20 years old. This same message which I earlier abhorred, by now became a constant irritant to my mind and I wanted to get a final answer from somewhere.

So, I decided to keep it in a secret prayer to the unknown living God. Months later in a miraculous way, I was affirmed regarding this truth from another source. Well I decided to read the Holy Bible which I never did before. Surprisingly a brother called Sam Daniel from Christ Church said he will be glad to teach me the chapters on revelation.

The day I started these lessons I never thought in my wildest dreams that one day I could become a born-again Christian. It initially occurred to me that the concept of being born again means rigid concepts that are difficult to follow. The thought that you need to be Christlike is even more petrifying as you just can't be so good is what strikes you first. But by Gods grace, the grace concept came in and it taught the fact that a Christian cannot be Christlike overnight but there is a need to grow day by day till one completes his/her final journey to an unknown place. Growing up! I did not fathom the depth of that growth until I watched my son grow. I understood that you need the help of God Himself to overcome the first few years like how a baby needs its mother and later on all those problems of growing up is exactly a struggle to reach where you are. You have the freedom to fall, but you need the courage to ask God to help you instead of you solving it.

The first phase is knowing God, the second one is accepting God and third one is having a covenant with God, the fourth one is practical living and finally to be Christlike. Now this process of going through these stages is like gold purified in fire. The more you want to be Christlike the more accountable your actions are. I learned that to be Christlike you need to know the likes of heavenly Father. Now the question came, how to know what the Father likes. The Holy Bible teaches us on lots of life stories, commandments, what to do for practical living etc. Now one group believes that grace is enough to see you through God, know your problems and God will understand your shortcomings and carry you through. Is sinning always ok to God? Now I sat for many days to know

What God loves and What God hates? I started reading the Bible and marking out all the areas from New and Old Testaments about the various Sins recorded in the Bible. This journey was to find out What God expects from the man? Every person claiming to be a child of God is taken through different growth stages before he becomes Christlike or is in the process of being Christlike. God always had an ideal instruction manual in mind but as man always deviates from what is good, the instruction manual is no more valid and God takes charge as a repairer and takes him through various stages of repair till he becomes good and functional. Some machines cannot be repaired and ultimately become scrap or are totally destroyed and burned. If you don't follow the instruction manual then you need to be ready for trouble shooting followed by a period of uselessness and anxiety. This book is an onward journey to reveal the likes and dislikes of God. This book is just an attempt to point out the perfectness of God and the discipline and orderliness God expects a man to possess. Yet it is difficult to practically follow or understand certain aspects. But the Holy Spirit, our mentor and guide leads us and helps us to achieve what we consider impossible. Some points in the book could seem extremely conservative, not modern or suitable to the present style of living in this day and age. But if it pleases God then why not attempt to do so, at least by keeping the matters that you think you cannot do in prayer. If you enquire with God, with all your heart and soul on all matters regarding great or small things, God teaches you and helps you in making a decision. While attempting to point out the perfectness of God the reader is reminded that this is what God loves us to be like but your circumstances might be totally different and God might be dealing with you in a different way.

Finally a word on why *Pandora's Box of 101 Sins* was chosen as the title. This entire book was framed during my quiet time with the Lord, after completing the book when I counted the Sins it totalled 101. I kept the title after putting the same in prayer. Though I received many criticisms from my friends for the present title I resolved to go by the same as it was after praying, this title was selected. The Holy Spirit is the one who convicts us of what displeases God hence the reader is requested to go through this book and to finally analyze if he is contended and happy in the Lord. Hope you enjoy reading this book and may you find a new beginning in your life, a walk closer with God.

Dr. Lovely

Contents

Section 3

SINS AGAINST SELF

Section 4

CONCLUSION

Section 1
SINS AGAINST GOD

Introduction

Both Adam and Eve were born in the glory of God and had a close relationship with Him, yet they sinned. Why did it happen and What are the chances of true believers not sinning?

The father of sin is disobedience and the mother of sin is idolatry. If we take a closer look at what happened to Eve, we would find that, before Eve sinned, the first thing that could have happened was that she distanced herself from communicating with God frequently as before. The time she spent in the company of God lessened and she started to remain in solitude for hours. This provided Satan the opportunity to sow the seeds of sin. He observed that she was alone and her thoughts could be easily influenced. Without God's companionship her mind was weak and Satan approached her because she gave the chance by remaining lonely and away from God. As long as Eve remained in close communion with God, the devil did not have access to her, but when she started to drift away from God, she lost her sense of reasoning, and therefore succumbed to the sin. The very minute she started to converse, listen, and enjoy Satan's companionship, she failed her test. No man can serve two masters. If you do not keep away from evil people, and fail to communicate with God from time to time, you become vulnerable or closer to sin than you imagine. Eve's mistake of listening to Lucifer opened the way to evil thoughts and finally she took the step to sin. Not only did she eat the forbidden fruit, she also gave it to her husband. This is what happens to believers who do not persevere in prayer. Prayer moves a believer closer to God while sin is a separation from God. We must spend time with the Lord. Once we stop spending this peaceful time with God, we start becoming like Eve. If we get so busy with our daily lives that we spend less and less time with God, this creates an avenue for sin to set in by taking charge of our minds.

All sins are destructive, with eternal consequences when unconfessed, if one does not seek forgiveness or have a repentant heart. However, all types of sins are taken care of at the cross, where the power of sin is broken by the eternal work of redemption of our Lord Jesus Christ.

This section of the book highlights the eternal commandments and its significance, and how sin becomes unforgivable. God pardons sins if you genuinely ask for forgiveness. However, you need to genuinely repent for your sins and not simply ask for forgiveness. Because asking for forgiveness without regret is like a thorn in the flesh, it pricks you all your life till you die. Let us have the wisdom to choose the right path filled with peace and understanding.

What are the sins against God?

The foremost sin in our life is when we do not acknowledge the presence of God. The next problem is we acknowledge but we do not live by the commandments set forth in the holy book. The concept of eliminating all laws and existing on only the guidance of Holy Spirit is a good idea provided you know that the entire holy book is more strongly confirmed by the spirit of God and not eliminated.

In brief the sins against God can be categorized as

- Disobedience to the Ten Commandments
- Disobedience to instructions from God
- Idol worship
- Vanity and pride
- Witch Craft/Sorcery/Divination/Enchantments
- Adultery
- Questioning/Cursing/Complaining against God
- Blasphemy/Mocking/Rebuking Holy spirit/ Altering/forming new commandments as per the convenience of man

- Eating the blood of any living animal
- Denying God/ Not God fearing
- Not Standing for God/ Not Testifying God
- Not giving Tithe

1

Disobedience to the Commandments

Every sin starts with disobedience. That's why it's termed as the *father of sins*. A disobedient person might be lazy, careless, or stubborn. Stubborn people have a lesser chance to inherit the eternal life because they know the truth but never accept it. A lazy person's mind is willing to do the right thing but he is too lazy to do it. A careless person is inconsistent in obedience. The mind to obey is a gift from God and if you do not have an obedient nature you should ask God to help you obey His commandments. It was God's commandment to Adam and Eve not to eat from the tree of good and evil. Eve disobeyed God's commandment and lost eternal life. As a result she was cursed with sorrow, pain at childbirth, and a dominating husband. And because Adam listened to his wife, and disobeyed God, the ground was hardened and he had to toil hard for his daily food. Earlier, by God's grace, food was available easily and for free, but now Adam faced a lot of difficulties to earn his daily meal. As a result of disobedience to commandment, death overpowered them (*Gen 3:16 to19*). Due to the sin of disobedience, man lost his glory and became mortal. There are many examples in the Bible where disobedience to other commandments by God led to some form of punishments. Saul also lost his kingship due to disobedience (*1sa 13:11-14).*

The Ten Commandments are eternal and were given to Moses by God. All other laws of New Testament are based on these commandments (*Deu 5:7 to 21*).

- There is only one God
- Man is not to worship any image in any form or make them
- Not to take the name of the Lord in vain
- To keep the Sabbath day holy (Referred to as seventh day in Bible)
- To honour thy father and mother
- Not to kill
- Not to commit adultery
- Not to steal
- Not to bear false witness against thy neighbor
- Not to covet thy neighbor's wealth.

The above commandments are everlasting. The everlasting commandments from the Old Testament are repeated in the New Testament and are enforced strongly.

Rom 13:9 for this, Thou shalt not commit adultery, Thou shalt not kill, Thou shalt not steal, Thou shalt not bear false witness, Thou shalt not covet; and if there be any other commandment, it is briefly comprehended in this saying, namely, Thou shalt love thy neighbor as thyself.

Blessings for following the Ten Commandments:

- God will bless the generation of those who hold on to the Commandments
- God will avenge your enemies
- God's mercy will continue forever
- You shall be blessed and there will be no one barren or childless
- All that you do will be blessed, your children, your land, your projects, your business, and anything else
- No sicknesses or plague shall visit you (*Deu 7:12-15*).

The above verses clearly indicate the significance of commandments. It is the duty of mankind to follow the everlasting commandments of God and in return, his life on earth is meant to be fruitful. The obedient person will be blessed and promises of a happy life for years to come are guaranteed. Hence, there is a need to follow all the eternal Ten Commandments faithfully. Are you barren, are you sick, are you depressed, are you taking sleeping pills, are you unsuccessful in whatever you do, are you unhappy, does the thought of suicide cross your mind, are you a slave to weaknesses as alcohol and sex? All of these are traceable to one origin; sin, which in itself is disobedience to the commandment of God at the beginning of creation.

However, you must understand that obedience of God's commandments is not instinctive. Man, by nature is sinful; the natural man cannot obey God's law by his own power. When the passions of a man are derived from his love for God and dependence on his creator, there is a motivation from within that man (spirit of man) to please God and obey Him.

That is why the Bible says in Pro 20:27 that *the spirit of man [is] the candle of the LORD, searching all the inward parts of the belly.* In the same vein, the word of God also states in Job 32:8 that *[there is] a spirit in man: and the inspiration of the almighty giveth them understanding.*

The story of the rich young ruler, (MK10:17-22) illustrates our point here. Despite keeping all the commandments, he lacked one essential thing: his love for his earthly possessions had beclouded his love for God. When he was told to choose his creator instead of his wealth, he went away sad. That shows that his obedience of the commandments was not driven by his love of God, rather, it was simply an act of fulfilling the dictates of the law, which of course is hypocrisy. These examples of people in the Bible who disobeyed God and faced grave consequences are to remind us not to fall in the same trap and bear the burden of punishments related to each type of disobedience. To conclude here, any person following the commandments and living by it is a blessed and peaceful man. Such a man is well pleasing to God and he is led, guided, and protected by God till the end of his life.

Law and commandment holy:

Rom 7:12: Wherefore the law is holy, and the commandment holy, and just, and good.

Rom 7:13: Was then that which is good made death unto me? God forbid. But sin, that it might appear sin, working death in me by that which is good; that sin by the commandment might become exceeding sinful.

SABBATH---A neglected commandment

The Sabbath specifically mentioned as the seventh day comes under the everlasting commandments, which is not to change. When God created heaven and earth he rested on the seventh day, the Saturday. However, the believers in the New Testament worship on the first day of week. The death and resurrection of Jesus fulfills and abolishes all the festivals feasts, and rituals, not the Ten Commandments. Many theories related to the resurrection of Jesus have been studied in depth. The New Testament belief of resurrection on Sunday morning and crucifixion on Friday cannot be related to the text Jonah in whales belly for three days and three nights hence a thorough study in this aspect need to be done.

Many theologians are of the opinion that the crucifixion was on Wednesday and the resurrection on Saturday noon. (John 20:19—Refers to the same day at evening meaning Saturday eve). Hence the true knowledge of what is right and wrong can be understood only when the spirit of the Lord works while reading the word of God. Hence I leave this thought to the reader to learn further. But the essence of Christianity lays not in vain theologies but true love for God and man. Let not these minor differences separate us from the love of God. But let us keep every day holy unto the Lord not just the Saturday and Sunday

Although I worship on Sundays, I try to keep the Saturday for religious activities such as prayer meetings and Godly work. After reading the Bible closely, I could not find a single verse that says Saturday is abolished and need not be considered as a holy day. The Sabbaths mentioned in some areas of Bible are festival Sabbaths.

Apart from the commandment Sabbath, the festival Sabbaths are no more. But let's not make an issue out of it and be more rigid than it is meant to be. I know in the Gulf countries, Friday is a holiday so Christians use that opportunity to worship and they work on all the days of the week. Hence, I recommend the readers to perform an in-depth study about Sabbath day.

Why I was attracted to Sabbath?

- Jesus himself kept the Sabbath without the external show off as the Pharisees did.
- Lord said that Sabbath is a day to do well and worship the Lord.
- Mighty God, the creator, rested on Sabbath as an example for others to follow.
- When all the other Ten Commandments are still being followed Why eliminate only the Sabbath out of the everlasting commandments?
- The resurrection day corresponds to the Sabbath. Though the Pharisees and Sadducees burdened everyone on Sabbath traditionally; Sabbath indicates a day to rest in the Lord, follow all that Jesus proved and taught. It is not just another day; it is the time to be spent with God, to thank Him for his mercies. The Old Testament has kept blessings for observing the Sabbath with true repentant heart and a thankful spirit to God and punishment for not observing Sabbath.

Punishment for not obeying Sabbath:

Famine

Losing children

Death

Widows at early age

Enslavement (Jer 17:21 to 24 and Jer 18:16 to 21).

Blessing for observing Sabbath:

Delighting the Lord

Ride upon high places of earth

Feed thee with heritage of Jacob

Bring to Holy Mountain and make them joyful

God will accept all their prayers

Isa 58:13: If thou turn away thy foot from the sabbath, from doing thy pleasure on my holy day; and call the sabbath a delight, the holy of the LORD, honourable; and shalt honour him, not doing thine own ways, nor finding thine own pleasure, nor speaking thine own words.

Isa 58:14: Then shalt thou delight thyself in the LORD; and I will cause thee to ride upon the high places of the earth, and feed thee with the heritage of Jacob thy father: for the mouth of the LORD hath spoken it.

Now Sabbath is not only meant for Israelites but also Gentiles and strangers as indicated in the verses below.

Isa 56: 6: Also the sons of the stranger, that join themselves to the LORD, to serve him, and to love the name of the LORD, to be his servants, every one that keepeth the sabbath from polluting it, and taketh hold of my covenant.

Sabbath for the fields too:

God cares for everyone in his plan. He wants your servants and animals to rest, and therefore, he has asked you to follow this commandment. You may sow seeds in your land and reap its fruits for six years, but during the seventh year, you must leave the field as it is. This commandment for the land might be to replenish the land of its lost fertility of soil.

The God who made all things knows how much each of his creations can withstand and when they need rest. The close reading of the Bible shows that the yield they collected by following Sabbath for the land was plenty.

The Bible reveals the fact that Israel didn't keep this commandment for 140 years and had to be in exile for 70 years, that is 70 Sabbaths.

Exo 23:10: And six years thou shalt sow thy land, and shalt gather in the fruits thereof.

Exo 23:1: But the seventh year thou shalt let it rest and lie still; that the poor of thy people may eat: and what they leave the beasts of the field shall eat. In like manner thou shalt deal with thy vineyard, and with thy olive yard.

Exo 23:12: Six days thou shalt do thy work, and on the seventh day thou shalt rest: that thine ox and thine ass may rest, and the son of thy handmaid, and the stranger, may be refreshed.

Sabbath in New Testament:

Christ is the Lord of Sabbath, and Sabbath can be used to do God's work and good deeds that could benefit others, such as helping them in cases of emergency. Again, Christ said that Sabbath was made for man, but Christ never said Sabbath is abolished or that you don't need to keep it holy.

Mat 12:8: For the Son of man is Lord even of the Sabbath day.

Mat 12:11: And he said unto them, What man shall there be among you, that shall have one sheep, and if it fall into a pit on the Sabbath day, will he not lay hold on it, and lift it out?

Mat 12:12: How much then is a man better than a sheep? Wherefore it is lawful to do well on the Sabbath days.

Mar 2:27: And he said unto them, The Sabbath was made for man, and not man for the Sabbath:

Mar 2:28: Therefore the Son of man is Lord also of the Sabbath.

Mar 3:4: And he saith unto them, Is it lawful to do good on the Sabbath days, or to do evil? to save life, or to kill? But they held their peace.

Heb 4:4: For he hath said somewhere of the seventh day on this wise, And God rested on the seventh day from all his works;

So if God rested on the seventh day then man also needs to rest and follow the blessings God has kept in store. Ask God to teach us the exact way of what is right and God shall enlighten you through the Holy Spirit on what is the truth.

Disobedience to Instructions from God to Man

Apart from the Ten Commandments, the other instruction to believers through the life of Jesus Christ is to be baptized in the name of father son and Holy Spirit and to partake in the Lord's Supper in remembrance of our Lord.

What are the essential things for Christians?

A New Testament believer need to accept Jesus has his saviour and by accepting Jesus, he is led by the Holy Spirit in prayer and supplication to fulfill all the commandments. The sign that he is a believer is that he is baptized and is living a life on Christian principles (has testimony of man and God).

Baptism:

It is mandatory to follow the Ten Commandments. To instill and naturally follow them you need to believe that Jesus is the only way to salvation. Once you accept Jesus as your saviour and enter into a covenant with God through adult baptism you receive the guidance of Holy Spirit, your spiritual guide within your heart in all matters. Holy Spirit warns you of sin, danger and lack of prayer.

Mat 20:23: And he saith unto them, "Ye shall drink indeed of my cup, and be baptized with the baptism that I am baptized with: but to sit on my right hand, and on my left, is not mine to give, but *it shall be given to them* for whom it is prepared of my Father".

Remembering the Lord through breaking of bread:

To renew your heart constantly with God you partake in the breaking of bread by rechecking your commitment with the Lord every time you take part in the Lord's Table. The punishment for believers who partake of the Lords table with sin is sickness and sleep (death).

1Co 11:26: For as often as ye eat this bread, and drink the cup, ye proclaim the Lord's death till he come.

1Co 11:28: But let a man prove himself, and so let him eat of the bread, and drink of the cup.

1Co 11:29: For he that eateth and drinketh, eateth and drinketh judgment unto himself, if he discern not the body.

1Co 11:30: For this cause many among you are weak and sickly, and not a few sleep.

Do not follow after men's doctrines:

In God everything is made and done with perfection. Many of the customs followed in our lives are dictated by the traditions of men. We follow rituals with no meaning. These are the so called man made doctrines that make us superstitious of days and times. We hesitate to start a job at certain time of the day considers the stars and believe in superstition as our ancestors did. Our God does not burden us with rituals and times. If you love God and obey him with all your heart no day or time is bad.

Col 2:20: If ye died with Christ from the rudiments of the world, why, as though living in the world, do ye subject yourselves to ordinances,

Mar 7:7: Howbeit in vain do they worship me, teaching *for* doctrines the commandments of men.

Mar 7:8: For laying aside the commandment of God, ye hold the tradition of men, *as* the washing of pots and cups: and many other such like things ye do.

Mar 7:9: And he said unto them, "Full well ye reject the commandment of God, that ye may keep your own tradition".

Commandments for the benefit of man's health:

- Do not eat certain animals and fishes
- Do not eat dead animals
- Do not eat blood of any living thing

Types of Animals to consume:

In New Testament, the dream that Peter had was related to the acceptance of Gentiles into the God's kingdom, which is why Peter says later about Cornelius, that what God has made to be pure, how can you call unclean. It was regarding the Gentiles and not meant as a license to consume anything considered impure. The Old Testament clearly indicates what kind of food is edible and good for mankind. If you feel like eating things considered as impure and if you have no concern for health problems later on, you may go ahead and eat them.

While God says that it's not good for you, some New Testament believers claim that what matters is not what goes in but only what comes out and besides if you bless the food and eat, everything is purified. If in some areas you only get rat meat, you bless it and eat it. Well, I couldn't. What God says is impure for you is not good for you. God who made the body knows what is consumable and what is not. The manual of God clearly states what is harmful and what is not. You may either choose to follow the manual of your creator, or otherwise ignore it and suffer from unknown ailments while consuming the medications that the doctors prescribe and pray that you are saved from the adverse effects of these medications. If you are adamant to fill petrol in a diesel engine what could happen?

Lev 11:5: And the coney, because he cheweth the cud, but divideth not the hoof; he *is* unclean unto you.

Lev 11:6: And the hare, because he cheweth the cud, but divideth not the hoof; he *is* unclean unto you.

Lev 11:7: And the swine, though he divide the hoof, and be clovenfooted, yet he cheweth not the cud; he *is* unclean to you.

Lev 11:8: Of their flesh shall ye not eat, and their carcase shall ye not touch; they *are* unclean to you.

Lev 11:9: These shall ye eat of all that *are* in the waters: whatsoever hath fins and scales in the waters, in the seas, and in the rivers, them shall ye eat.

Lev 11:10 And all that have not fins and scales in the seas, and in the rivers, of all that move in the waters, and of any living thing which is in the waters, they shall be an abomination unto you:

Lev 11:11: They shall be even an abomination unto you; ye shall not eat of their flesh, but ye shall have their carcases in abomination.

Lev 11:12: Whatsoever hath no fins nor scales in the waters, that *shall be* an abomination unto you.

Lev 11:13: And these *are they which* ye shall have in abomination among the fowls; they shall not be eaten, they *are* an abomination: the eagle, and the ossifrage, and the ospray,

Lev 11:14: And the vulture, and the kite after his kind;

Lev 11:15: Every raven after his kind;

Lev 11:16: And the owl, and the night hawk, and the cuckow, and the hawk after his kind,

Lev 11:17: And the little owl, and the cormorant, and the great owl,

Lev 11:18: And the swan, and the pelican, and the gier eagle,

Lev 11:19: And the stork, the heron after her kind, and the lapwing, and the bat.

Lev 11:20: All fowls that creep, going upon *all* four, *shall be* an abomination unto you.

Lev 11:21: Yet these may ye eat of every flying creeping thing that goeth upon *all* four, which have legs above their feet, to leap withal upon the earth;

Lev 11:22: *Even* these of them ye may eat; the locust after his kind, and the bald locust after his kind, and the beetle after his kind, and the grasshopper after his kind.

Lev 11:23: But all *other* flying creeping things, which have four feet, *shall be* an abomination unto you.

Should not eat dead animals:

Bible repeatedly says dead animals should not be consumed. Well, the reason could be that the blood gets clotted inside a dead animal, which is not to be consumed; and also it gets putrefied making it unfit for consumption. All sorts of infectious diseases can stem out of it.

Exo 22:31: And ye shall be holy men unto me: neither shall ye eat *any* flesh *that is* torn of beasts in the field; ye shall cast it to the dogs.

Regarding touching of dead things:

This indicates the amount of hygiene man is required to have in order to have good health. Any dead animal or man can carry germs that can cause ill health in a living person. Hence Biblical commandments take care not only of a man's soul, but also the body he lives in. Man just needs to follow what is written in the word of God (Lev 11: 25-40).

2

Idolatry

What God hates the most is idol worship and bowing to the image or idols that are handmade.

Idols are made of mud, iron, gold and silver; designed by humans and worshiped by men. They have no eyes to see, no ears to hear, no voice to speak and are dead as the materials used to make them. How can anyone worship them? It is just a ritual and at the end of the day all your problems remain. The mighty God who's the Spirit and truth can hear us, protect us, speak to us, and besides we can feel our God in our day to day life. The result of worshiping the true and mighty God in spirit and truth guarantees peace in our hearts, confidence that God will manage and take us safely through all the trials of this world and will make our end beautiful.

Hab 2:18: What profiteth the graven image that the maker thereof hath graven it; the molten image, and a teacher of lies, that the maker of his work trusteth therein, to make dumb idols?

Hab 2:19: Woe unto him that saith to the wood, Awake; to the dumb stone, Arise, it shall teach! Behold, it *is* laid over with gold and silver, and *there is* no breath at all in the midst of it.

Idol worship includes:

- Images /photographs/people/any object you bow to
- Power and money/Influence
- Giving respect to men more than God

- Loving Job, riches, children, hobbies, and friends, display of wealth, family name position and status above God is idol worship. Worshipping figures of male or female objects, any beast or bird that flies; any reptiles or fish, sun, moon or stars or heavenly being is Idol worship.

Deu 4:16: Lest ye corrupt *yourselves,* and make you a graven image, the similitude of any figure, the likeness of male or female,

Deu 4:17: The likeness of any beast that *is* on the earth, the likeness of any winged fowl that flieth in the air,

Deu 4:18: The likeness of anything that creepeth on the ground, the likeness of any fish that *is* in the waters beneath the earth:

Deu 4:19: And lest thou lift up thine eyes unto heaven, and when thou seest the sun, and the moon, and the stars, *even* all the host of heaven, shouldest be driven to worship them, and serve them, which the LORD thy God hath divided unto all nations under the whole heaven.

Punishment:

- War and enslavement
- Subject to lack of freedom
- Withholding of heavenly blessings
- Losing of land, property, wife and children
- Encountering many stumbling blocks in life as diseases, worries, jail, anxieties, depression and loss of blessing to coming generations.
- Unnatural liking of male to male and female to female.
- Finally hell is the place you will reside.

Following are the supporting verses:

Jer 7:9: Will ye steal, murder, and commit adultery, and swear falsely, and burn incense unto Baal, and walk after other Gods whom ye know not;

Jer 7:18: The children gather wood, and the fathers kindle the fire, and the women knead *their* dough, to make cakes to the queen of heaven, and to pour out drink offerings unto other Gods, that they may provoke me to anger.

Because of idol worship God let Israelites as slaves to other nations and they suffered under the heavy hand of their enemies.

Jer 5:25: Your iniquities have turned away these *things,* and your sins have with holden good *things* from you.

Jer 6:12: And their houses shall be turned unto others, *with their* fields and wives together: for I will stretch out my hand upon the inhabitants of the land, saith the LORD.

Jer 6:21: Therefore thus saith the LORD, Behold, I will lay stumbling blocks before this people, and the fathers and the sons together shall fall upon them; the neighbour and his friend shall perish.

Rom 1:23: And changed the glory of the uncorruptible God into an image made like to corruptible man, and to birds, and four footed beasts, and creeping things.

Rom 1:24: Wherefore God also gave them up to uncleanness through the lusts of their own hearts, to dishonour their own bodies between themselves:

Rom 1:25: Who changed the truth of God into a lie, and worshipped and served the creature more than the Creator, who is blessed forever. Amen.

Exo 32:35: And the LORD plagued the people, because they made the calf, which Aaron made.

Exo 34:7: Keeping mercy for thousands, forgiving iniquity and transgression and sin, and that will by no means clear *the guilty;* visiting the iniquity of the fathers upon the children, and upon the children's children, unto the third and to the fourth *generation.*

Idolatry as per New Testament:

Regarding believers it is written that they should

2Co 6:14: Be not unequally yoked with unbelievers: for what fellowship have righteousness and iniquity? or what communion hath light with darkness?

2Co 6:15: And what concord hath Christ with Belial? or what portion hath a believer with an unbeliever?

2Co 6:16: And what agreement hath a temple of God with idols? for we are a temple of the living God; even as God said, I will dwell in them, and walk in them; and I will be their God, and they shall be my people.

1Co 10:14: Wherefore, my beloved, flee from idolatry.

1Co 10:20: But *I say*, that the things which the Gentiles sacrifice, they sacrifice to demons, and not to God: and I would not that ye should have communion with demons.

1Co 10:21: Ye cannot drink the cup of the Lord, and the cup of demons: ye cannot partake of the table of the Lord, and of the table of demons.

1Co 10:7: Neither be ye idolaters, as were some of them; as it is written, The people sat down to eat and drink, and rose up to play.

Concerning things sacrificed to idols:

1Co 8:1: Now concerning things sacrificed to idols: We know that we all have knowledge. Knowledge puffeth up, but love edifieth.

1Co 8:4: Concerning therefore the eating of things sacrificed to idols, we know that no idol is *anything* in the world, and that there is no God but one.

1Co 8:5: For though there be that are called Gods, whether in heaven or on earth; as there are Gods many, and lords many;

1Co 8:6: yet to us there is one God, the Father, of whom are all things, and we unto him; and one Lord, Jesus Christ, through whom are all things, and we through him.

1Co 8:10: for if a man see thee who hast knowledge sitting at meat in an idol's temple, will not his conscience, if he is weak, be emboldened to eat things sacrificed to idols?

1Co 8:11: For through thy knowledge he that is weak perisheth, the brother for whose sake Christ died.

Conclusion of whole matter:

Isa 2:18: And the idols he shall utterly abolish

Rev 14:9: And another angel, a third, followed them, saying with a great voice, If any man worshippeth the beast and his image, and receiveth a mark on his forehead, or upon his hand,

Rev 14:10: he also shall drink of the wine of the wrath of God, which is prepared unmixed in the cup of his anger; and he shall be tormented with fire and brimstone in the presence of the holy angels, and in the presence of the Lamb:

Exo 22:20: He that sacrificeth unto *any* God, save unto the LORD only, he shall be utterly destroyed.

Exo 23:13: And in all *things* that I have said unto you be circumspect: and make no mention of the name of other Gods, neither let it be heard out of thy mouth.

3

Vanity

The very sin that made the devil. A sin that hides within every ambitious person. How do you and I know that this sin lurks within us? It's easy to identify pride. The thoughts in your mind give us the clue to this grave disease pride. What are these thoughts? Here is a sample list of them for you to know.

Why the hell should I listen to someone who is much junior, my maid or a humble elder even though they may be correct?

Why should I hold an umbrella for this person working in my office holding a menial job?

Why should I make tea or coffee for my tired maid let her make it on her own?

Why should I take advice from my children or my subordinate I have the ability and brains to decide?

Why should I listen to my higher authorities when I can execute and do a better job than them?

The thoughts go on---now an intelligent observant and silent listener is able to pinpoint these people. They just need to start speaking and you know. The commonest dialogues go this way. I am a favorite in my office I can do everything better than others. I stand out prominent everywhere I go. I have enough money for another eight generations to live. I come from a royal family and belong to this family name; I am highly qualified and have better common sense than most of my colleagues. The list is endless.

Now just introspect on your daily thoughts and how you talk to others. A Godly person tends to enquire of the other persons health and his sufferings and prays about it and also gives a patient hearing to what others have to say. A proud person ridicules, mocks, teases and often passes slide remarks hurting other people's feelings. If you possess pride you really need to ask Jesus to touch you or else you become a secret pain in the neck to community and people around you.

2Th 2:4: he that opposeth and exalteth himself against all that is called God or that is worshipped; so that he sitteth in the temple of God, setting himself forth as God.

2Th 2:8: And then shall be revealed the lawless one, whom the Lord Jesus shall slay with the breath of his mouth, and bring to nought by the manifestation of his coming;

Factors related to pride:

- Considering one to be self-made
- Glorifying one above God
- Proud look and thoughts
- Giving more time and effort to ourselves to make one rich, for beauty and education while neglecting others
- Bloating in self with pride in heart and eyes.

Vanity can lead to a debacle. A man who thinks he knows everything, never bothers to take advice or discuss matters with wiser people, might fall into trouble. He might fight, talk rudely, and ridicule people. He might put down others ideas, never let anyone excel above himself, and try to dominate the scene. As a result, people might hate him and talk behind his back.

Types of Pride as related to Bible:

Vain imagination:

Are evil thoughts that are of no use to any one is self destructive and over a period of time can cause harm to others. They include thoughts that can harm others, thoughts to overpower or exercise authority over others. Because the man was full of evil thoughts God repented why he ever created man (Gen 6:3-7). The result of evil imagination is that life gets shorter and shorter, man falls prey to diseases.

***Self praise*:**

Every achievement, in this world can puff up humans. A man who is puffed up cannot stop speaking about himself. In every word he utters the 'I' stands prominent; *I did this and that*. Every action of his speaks of his puffed up attitude. He claims that his inventions are great and beneficial; he is proud and believes that no other person is like him. He claims to be an extremely wealthy, intelligent and great man.

A person who imagines to be superior in all aspects above all others, who takes credits for all his assets and education, is provoking God to anger. Man was made in the form and image of God to give glory to God and not to glorify his achievements above God. Self praise is to trumpet on his achievements or assets quite often in public gatherings.

1Ti 6:4: he is puffed up, knowing nothing, but doting about questionings and disputes of words, whereof cometh envy, strife, railings, evil surmisings,

Dan 5:20: But when his heart was lifted up, and his mind hardened in pride, he was deposed from his kingly throne, and they took his glory from him:

Self exaltation:

God is powerful; we can never be like Him. We are his creations. No creation can equal the creator. Everything is subject to God's authority. Any man who thinks he is greater and more glorious than God will have a fate similar to Lucifer the angel. Encouraging others to consider you as a superhuman or equal to God is a great sin.

Act 12:21: And upon a set day Herod, arrayed in royal apparel, sat upon his throne, and made an oration unto them.

Act 12:22: And the people gave a shout, *saying, It is* the voice of a God, and not of a man.

Act 12:23: And immediately the angel of the Lord smote him, because he gave not God the glory: and he was eaten of worms, and gave up the ghost.

Self righteous:

A man who believes that only hard work is sufficient for success is a fool because one cannot even move a finger of his hand without God's decision. A man who donated a substantial amount of money to an orphanage should know that God helped him to earn it. It's like a tree proud of its fruits with no thought for its roots. A self-righteous man is the same. (Job's friends)

Now, in conclusion of this chapter here is a great king who understood that God is able to raise the poor and weakest and bring down high looks.

Dan 4:37: Now I Nebuchadnezzar praise and extol and honour the King of heaven, all whose works *are* truth, and his ways judgment: and those that walk in pride he is able to abase.

4

Witchcraft/Sorcery

Trying God can be knowing the right things to do but going after the worldly ways as astrology, blindly believing prophecies from anyone, man pleasing, vanity, idol worship and asking God for signs. If a man sins without knowing the true God it is better for him than knowing God and sinning. A back slider will be judged more than the Atheist.

Various people who try God:

False Christians -are people who claim to be close to God yet in their true lives they are away from God. These so called Christians act as if they are the holiest people living and God hears only their prayers. They conveniently give their ideas as God given ideas and lure people to act through their guidance without even asking God.

They are Christians who claim that they pray for your matters in need with earnestness but don't do so and some of them on meeting a new person also makes promises as "don't worry all things are going to be ok I will pray for you -- but never remember the matter after that incident. In most of the cases when you encounter a healed brother/sister you tell him how much you prayed for his healing which you never even did once. All these things are going to be accounted one day. If you as a Christian cannot keep promises of prayer, do not talk.

Tit 1:16: They profess that they know God; but by their works they deny him, being abominable, and disobedient, and unto every good work reprobate.

False prophets: They prophesy whatever comes to their mind. They do not lead holy lives. The life of a false prophet can be filled with adultery, lies, and egos, filled with worldliness. Do not believe what they say. Know a man from what fruits he bears. If his/her life is a bad testimony and their behavior is not in par with the biblical standards do not believe in his/her prophecies (Jer 14:15,16, Mat 7:15,16, Mar 13:6,7,23).

Asking familiar spirits: Asking the spirit of the dead, revering the dead, worshipping the dead are all contrary to the biblical commandments. Most of the mental maniacs I have met were people who at least once tried to speak to spirits. Consequently, these evil spirits then take control of them.

1Sa 28:7: Then said Saul unto his servants, Seek me a woman that hath a familiar spirit, that I may go to her, and enquire of her. And his servants said to him, Behold, *there is* a woman that hath a familiar spirit at Endor. As known to all Saul already was troubled by evil spirit that made him behave abnormally.

Lev 19:31: Regard not them that have familiar spirits, neither seek after wizards, to be defiled by them: I *am* the LORD your God.

Divination and enchantments:

This is still a common practice in many parts of the world as walking over fire to appease Gods.

2Ki 17:17: And they caused their sons and their daughters to pass through the fire, and used divination and enchantments, and sold themselves to do evil in the sight of the LORD, to provoke him to anger.

2Ki 17:18: Therefore the LORD was very angry with Israel, and removed them out of his sight: there was none left but the tribe of Judah only.

Seers and diviners: Evil magic to harm others to find our future or to appease Gods are all evil and will lead to mental imbalance.

Even in today's age many woman are considered to be possessed and killed. Many kids just born are killed when diviners call them as a bad omen. People who predict the future, who give wrong council, are all hated by God.

Mic 5:12: And I will cut off witchcrafts out of thine hand; and thou shalt have no *more* soothsayers:

Whoredoms: Sacrificing lives to appease idols is called whoredom.

Eze 16:20: Moreover thou hast taken thy sons and thy daughters, whom thou hast borne unto me, and these hast thou sacrificed unto them to be devoured. *Is this* of thy whoredoms a small matter,

Deu 18:10: There shall not be found among you *any one* that maketh his son or his daughter to pass through the fire, *or* that useth divination, *or* an observer of times, or an enchanter, or a witch,

Deu 18:11: Or a charmer, or a consulter with familiar spirits, or a wizard, or a necromancer.

Deu 18:12: For all that do these things *are* an abomination unto the LORD: and because of these abominations the LORD thy God doth drive them out from before thee.

Witch craft:

Many rural areas have many people who are into black magic. They possess evil powers and can harm ordinary people not protected by the blood of Jesus. Death was the penalty for such people in Old Testament times.

Exo 22:18: Thou shalt not suffer a witch to live.

Lev 20:27: A man also or woman that hath a familiar spirit, or that is a wizard, shall surely be put to death: they shall stone them with stones: their blood *shall be* upon them.

Wizards:

Isa 8:19: And when they shall say unto you, Seek unto them that have familiar spirits, and unto wizards that peep, and that mutter: should not a people seek unto their God? for the living to the dead?

No man can ever predict the end except God; hence depend on God alone and not men who claim they are agents to God. If you listen to them and are misled then you are trying God.

One example I would like to cite here is the star signs. Many of the believers, on receiving the morning news paper turn to the star sign page to see how this week is going to be. This is also astrology. Believing in the star signs and the predictions for that week is ungodly.

5

Adultery

Today many individuals and nations support gay marriages and lesbian marriages. But what does the Bible say for these. The very sin Sodom and Gomorrah committed and perished as a nation. Does God deal with the same sin differently now. Nations who give approval to such acts better beware, the mighty God is watching you and the end is very soon to come. We are a spiritual body made in the image and glory of God. Any abuse to the body, in any form, is a direct insult to the mighty God. Committing adultery, with any other apart from the permitted man and woman relation are all against the commandment of God. The results of these sins are serious for the body and soul. The evil forces then act on you giving way to all the evil manifestations of this world.

Fornication:

1Th 4:3: for this is the will of God, *even* your sanctification, that ye abstain from fornication;

Most of the people who commit adultery are people who give no value to relationships. They don't love their children and are not concerned about their wellbeing. They don't know what they talk and are into drinks and drugs.

If any person commits adultery with your father, mother, brother, or sister it is an unforgivable sin. A husband or wife committing adultery with another while in a married relation is an unforgivable sin. Committing fornication before marriage is also a sin.

Adultery is an unforgivable sin and Bible recommends and advice on keeping away from such who commit adultery or tempts you to commit adultery (*Pro 5:8, Pro 2:16-20*).

Fornication with fathers wife (1Co 5:1, *Gen 35:22, Lev 20:11*).

Reuben slept with his father's wife and lost the blessings that he should have otherwise received. (*2Sa:16:21*). Absalom commits adultery with his father's wives and consequently he died (*2Sa:18:9*). And Absalom rode upon a mule, and the mule went under the thick boughs of a great oak, and his head caught hold of the oak, and he was taken up between the heaven and the earth; and the mule that *was* under him went away. What a way to die!

If you commit adultery with another man's wife, Old Testament gives the punishment of putting you to death, the man and woman (*Lev 20:10*).

If a man sleeps with his daughter, again death is the punishment for both as per Old Testament (Lot slept with his daughter and the whole of the nation that came of it, the Ammonites and Moabites were cursed forever. (*Lev 20:11*) If a man sleeps with another man death is the punishment (*Lev 20:12, 13*).

If a man sleeps with his wife and also wife's mother Old Testament says burn all three in fire. (*Lev 20:14*). God says all these are wicked things.

If a man or woman lies with an animal Bible says both the man/woman and animal should die. (*Lev 20:15, 16*). If a man sleeps with his sister he is to die (*2Sa 13:15, 16, ultimately Amnon is killed*) (*2Sa: 13:28*).

You shall not lie or see the nakedness of your mother, father, sister, father's sister, mothers sister, father's brother (or his wife), brother's wife, wife's sister, son's daughter, or daughter's daughter and neighbor's wife (*Lev 18: 7-22*).

You shall not lie with a woman during her period time (*Lev 18:19*).

It's an unforgivable sin to give your children to Gods and Goddesses (*Lev 18: 21*).

Believers marrying women who are not believers is a form of adultery as once you are baptized and taking communion with the Lord you are liable to keep your body holy and pure as a living sacrifice. Your marriage partner should also be holy and pure if not you are defiling your body with a strange woman and committing adultery. This strange woman will slowly eat into you like cancer and kill you totally as what happened to King Solomon.

"(**1Ki 11:1, 2, 3, 4**)" But King Solomon loved many strange women, together with the daughter of Pharaoh, women of the Moabites, Ammonites, Edomites, Zidonians, *and* Hittites).

"As King Solomon grew old, his heart" was turned from the true God and he lost communion with God. Once he lost communion with the Lord he started worshipping idols and Bible says he did evil in the sight of God and lost his kingdom.

1Ki 11:11: Wherefore the LORD said unto Solomon, Forasmuch as this is done of thee, and thou hast not kept my covenant and my statutes, which I have commanded thee, I will surely rend the kingdom from thee, and will give it to thy servant.

These above verses indicate clearly that God punishes people who sin but does not take away the blessings he promised his children. Till now all the verses quoted are from the Old Testament and a New Testament believer is likely to think that Jesus died for all sins hence it's ok to commit adultery and even if you do then just ask for forgiveness in the name of Jesus and all your sins would be washed away each time you do. The following verses clearly indicate the severity of New Testament in its condemnation of sexual immorality. It says that even by look or thoughts you are not to lust, leave alone sleeping with someone. Again New Testament goes one step further and tells that only one wife is permitted and if you divorce you cannot marry another man's wife, if so it's committing adultery.

Mat 5:27: Ye have heard that it was said by them of old time, Thou shalt not commit adultery

Mat 5:28: But I say unto you, That whosoever looketh on a woman to lust after her hath committed adultery with her already in his heart.

Luk 16:18: Whosoever putteth away his wife, and marrieth another, committeth adultery: and whosoever marrieth her that is put away from *her* husband committeth adultery.

Now to conclude the whole matter –

Until you marry with the right partner, God has prepared for you, it is you as a believer's duty to be chaste in body, thoughts and words. Once you are committed to a man or woman in marriage it's a lifelong commitment till death. You are to stay away from the partner only if the partner commits adultery with another or when it involves domestic violence. Apart from adultery all other matters can be settled by prayer, counseling and treatment even the mental or physical health.

Now if any man or constitution or nation supports any form of adultery as mentioned in this chapter, punishment from almighty is sure. The punishments mentioned in the Bible is that God is going to give away your children the same and take away the peace from your families. If the entire nation supports any form of adultery against the word of God, any of the following can happen: calamities, war, plagues and famine.

Lev 18:27: (For all these abominations have the men of the land done, which *were* before you, and the land is defiled;)

Lev 18:28: That the land spue not you out also, when ye defile it, as it spued out the nations that *were* before you.

Lev 18:29: For whosoever shall commit any of these abominations, even the souls that commit *them* shall be cut off from among their people.

Lev 18:30: Therefore shall ye keep mine ordinance, that *ye* commit not *any one* of these abominable customs, which were committed before you, and that ye defile not yourselves therein: I *am* the LORD your God.

Dear Brother/Sister if you have committed such sins in your life and seek genuine forgiveness from God look at the example of David. He committed a great sin but he took the punishment from God with grace and genuinely repented. Ask God to help you to be pure as God wishes, and submit all matters to God and God shall protect our mind and body. As far as a New Testament believer is concerned if you have committed any of the above sins there is still hope for you in Christ, who is able to cleanse us from all our sins and guilt and present us with purity to the heavenly father. Just accept Jesus Christ as your Lord and saviour.

6

Questioning/Cursing God

The first few chapters spoke about the everlasting Commandments and other laws required for peaceful living. There are several factors besides disobedience to the Commandments that displease God. This chapter will address them.

Murmuring Against God:

If some calamity or unwanted thing or tragedy strikes you, you are not supposed to blame God or say what was the use of praying. Praying is not a tool to please God. It's a way to know God's will; submit your life to God, hear God's still voice and praise God for all his mercies and kindness he has bestowed upon you. An ideal example is Job's life. He never even once murmured but kept saying "The *God who gave all to me also has the right to take everything away from me*", because of his unflinching faith God restored Job sevenfold.

Cursing/Questioning:

During the journey of Israelites from Egypt to the Promised Land, the human weaknesses were clearly exposed. They cursed and questioned God and God's anger killed them. Your life is God's creation; hence, the creator has the freedom to choose the manner in which your life should be led.

Picture this situation: you decide to create a garden and employ a gardener. However, the gardener is adamant to design the garden according to his likes and completely ignores your choices. He decides to plant only colorful leaves whereas you want flowering plants. What could you do in such a situation?

You would either dismiss the gardener, or get rid of his changes and instruct him to design according to your likes. If the gardener is a stubborn self-willed person he starts to curse you, complaint against you, murmur within him or decide not to work anymore for you or out rightly fight with you or abuse you with hurtful words, isn't this unreasonable. However, an intelligent gardener would first understand his master's likes, dislikes and plans. He would then sketch a garden map and submit to his master for feedback. On approval, he would immediately start work and keep his master informed of the progress. He would also work with utmost dedication, at a good pace, and seek for his master's opinion on the final work.

These people are called Godly children and God loves them and calls them dependable, accountable, reliable, faithful, truthful, and eligible for the ultimate crown. They are disciplined, hardworking, intelligent, and always listen to the quiet voice of God. No one would hire the initial foolish gardener even if he possesses the skills. This is what happens to people who don't follow the Commandments of the mighty Lord. There is a definite punishment for disobeying God. All plagues, calamities, pestilences, wars, diseases, unknown ailments are the results of complaining, disobedience and murmurings.

Num 14:12: I will smite them with the pestilence, and disinherit them, and will make of thee a greater nation and mightier than they.

Num 21:5: And the people spake against God, and against Moses, Wherefore have ye brought us up out of Egypt to die in the wilderness? for there is no bread, neither is there any water; and our soul loatheth this light bread.

Num 21:6: And the LORD sent fiery serpents among the people, and they bit the people; and much people of Israel died.

Num 11:1: And when the people complained, it displeased the LORD: and the LORD heard it; and his anger was kindled; and the fire of the LORD burnt among them, and consumed them that were in the uttermost parts of the camp.

Many times when we are in trouble; we curse God and question Him. We also tend to stop praying and forget that at times things happen for good.

We complain of the problem and get irritated thinking of the obstacles. We don't realize that God is protecting us from either losing eternal life or from Satan's trap. He knows our end.

Many times when I am in a hurry and land up in a traffic block, I think that God might have protected me from an accident that was due. The mighty God always stays by your side. If you are his child, you are protected. A fractured leg, binding us to bed or a sickness are all means to give your over-tired body adequate rest. If you have followed every page of the Bible, you will believe all things happen for a purpose. If you have not known God and if God loves you and wants you to know him, he might put you in trouble to bring you to the knowledge of God. If you are to face a tough situation later in life, God will put you through small situations to make you strong to face the upcoming struggle.

Disobedience to the choice of God

God gave Lot the option of going to the mountain but Lot chose the city by his own will and the result was sin.

Gen 19:19: Behold now, thy servant hath found grace in thy sight, and thou hast magnified thy mercy, which thou hast shewed unto me in saving my life; and I cannot escape to the mountain, lest some evil take me, and I die:

Gen 19:20: Behold now, this city is near to flee unto, and it is a little one: Oh, let me escape thither, (is it not a little one?) and my soul shall live.

Gen 19:36: Thus were both the daughters of Lot with child by their father.

In this world, we are free to choose our profession, job, business partners, etc. However, if you believe in God and consider him your good friend, you should discuss your decisions and choices with Him. If you choose with God's consent, you will be at peace in any situation you come across. However, if your decision is contrary to God's plan, sooner or later you will be at loss.

Displeased God

Gen 38:10: and the thing which he did displeased the LORD: wherefore he slew him also

When we do things contrary to what the Bible says you displease God. God has laid the Commandments and some basic rules for human life. These are foundations on which you should build your life; anything against this displeases God.

Disobedience to God's order/work:

Many times you are clearly instructed to do certain things by God yet you fail to do it the way God wants you to.

This is clear disobedience of God's order. God commands you to pray for a specific purpose or you are heavily burdened to do a Godly job but a sudden worldly appointment can make you give God a second preference.

Jon1:15: So they took up Jonah, and cast him forth into the sea: and the sea ceased from her raging.

Jon 1:17: Now the LORD had prepared a great fish to swallow up Jonah. And Jonah was in the belly of the fish three days and three nights.

Jon 2:1: Then Jonah prayed unto the LORD his God out of the fish's belly,

Jon 2:4: Then I said, I am cast out of thy sight; yet I will look again toward thy holy temple.

Disrespecting God

In Gods eyes there is a specific way to do everything. Let us consider few examples. When Moses saw the burning bush, unaware that it's a holy place he approached with his sandals, God commanded him to remove the same. Same way if you have to please God you need to do it the way God wants it to be done. Cain and Abel both brought sacrifices, God was pleased with Abel. Throughout the Bible God loves his children who respects and are fearful from him. It's our moral duty as the creation to love and respect the supreme creator. No man can force us to do it; it should come from within the heart. Wearing decent clothes, removing sandals, coming with a pure and thanks giving heart for the worship are all ways to respect God.

2Sa 6:7: And the anger of the LORD was kindled against Uzzah; and God smote him there for his error; and there he died by the ark of God.

Gen 4:5: But unto Cain and to his offering he had not respect. And Cain was very wroth, and his countenance fell.

How can we respect God

- Obeying the commandments.
- Asking God's opinion before making any decisions in your life.
- Thanking and praising God for all the goodness and mercies.
- Giving good testimony of our life to others.
- Keeping faith in the Lord and depending only on him.
- Not respecting or loving anyone above God.
- Accepting the will of God with gladness in tough situations also.
- Praying on Sabbath.
- Attending the service with prayer, respect as removing the sandals while attending service, wearing decent dress and simple in dressing.
- Attending service with clean heart and thanksgiving.

Do not swear:

Mat 5:34: But I say unto you, Swear not at all; neither by heaven; for it is God's throne:

Mat 5:35: Nor by the earth; for it is his footstool: neither by Jerusalem; for it is the city of the great King.

Mat 5:36: Neither shalt thou swear by thy head, because thou canst not make one hair white or black.

Mat 5:37: But let your communication be, Yea, yea; Nay, nay: for whatsoever is more than these cometh of evil.

7

Blasphemy/Mocking of Holy Spirit

What is Blasphemy: the act or offense of speaking sacrilegiously about God or sacred things; profane talk?

Lev 24:16: And he that blasphemeth the name of the LORD, he shall surely be put to death, and all the congregation shall certainly stone him: as well the stranger, as he that is born in the land, when he blasphemeth the name of the LORD, shall be put to death.

Few of the Blasphemies

- Not believing in Jesus as saviour.
- Believing that all Gods are same and one.
- Putting our mighty God along with idols.
- Mocking and rebuking God's word and not believing in it.
- Teaching or testifying against the word of God.

Unbelief in the holy words/Denying of God:

For those who say God doesn't exist and even if God does exist they refuse to believe the right way to worship God.

Luk 12:9: But he that denieth me before men shall be denied before the angels of God.

Luk 12:10: And whosoever shall speak a word against the Son of man, it shall be forgiven him: but unto him that blasphemeth against the Holy Ghost it shall not be forgiven.

8

Consuming Blood of any Living Thing in any Form

God has said blood is in life and you shall not eat blood. I have seen many dishes made with blood of animals alone. In fact, I have closely observed a family who used to consume the blood of goats and cow as delicacies. Most of them suffer from skin ailments and unknown depression. What God recommends as sin man dares not eat. If you do, you will never be able to live a free life in this world.

Lev 19:26: Ye shall not eat *anything* with the blood: neither shall ye use enchantment, nor observe times.

Lev 17:10: And whatsoever man *there be* of the house of Israel, or of the strangers that sojourn among you, that eateth any manner of blood; I will even set my face against that soul that eateth blood, and will cut him off from among his people.

Lev 17:11: For the life of the flesh *is* in the blood: and I have given it to you upon the altar to make an atonement for your souls: for it *is* the blood *that* maketh an atonement for the soul.

9

Not God-fearing

Subtly bringing in new doctrines and commandments that are men founded is equal to denying God. When you don't believe in Jesus Christ, baptism and Holy Spirit you are denying God.

Rev 22:18: I testify unto every man that heareth the words of the prophecy of this book, if any man shall add unto them, God shall add unto him the plagues which are written in this book.

Rev 22:19: And if any man shall take away from the words of the book of this prophecy, God shall take away his part from the tree of life, and out of the holy city, which are written in this book.

Not believing in Jesus as savior

The only way to salvation is by believing in Jesus send by God. Jesus was also sent to establish the laws and feasts of the Old Testament. By the birth and death of our Lord the entire Old Testament festivals and sacrificial laws were fulfilled and need not be followed. However, the Ten Commandments are ever-lasting, which needs to be followed till the end. As the sins of the world are too grievous, the almighty God cannot reach every human, hence Jesus is the mediator for all mankind. The way you think is influenced by the kind of life you lead, the people you move around with, your family, upbringing, knowledge and fear of God.

If your mind is filled with prayers, the Holy Spirit will lead you and no evil thoughts will have access to your mind. Guard your mind by constant prayer or you will succumb to thoughts of the devil. When you don't submit your life to God, results and the effects of sin manifests in your life. Every sin bears consequences, which come in the form of troubles, worries and sickness. If you are excessively worried about matters, you are away from God.

Isa 59:2: But your iniquities have separated between you and your God, and your sins have hid *his* face from you, that he will not hear.

Mar 8:38: Whosoever therefore shall be ashamed of me and of my words in this adulterous and sinful generation; of him also shall the Son of man be ashamed, when he cometh in the glory of his Father with the holy angels.

10

Testifying God

What are the matters that prove you are not standing with God: forsaking God, do not have the faith to believe his promises for you, you disapprove God's blessing, take God for granted, self planning against Gods will and not acknowledging Gods love and mercies. Let us also see few examples from the Bible.

Forsaking God

You once knew God so well like Eve, but all of a sudden you believe the lie of Satan and the world, forsaking God, to become of the world. The day you stop spending time with God, asking council from God; you have forsaken God.

Jer 8:9: The wise men are ashamed, they are dismayed and taken: lo, they have rejected the word of the LORD; and what wisdom is in them?

Jer 8:10: Therefore will I give their wives unto others, and their fields to them that shall inherit them: for everyone from the least even unto the greatest is given to covetousness, from the prophet even unto the priest every one dealeth falsely.

Jer 8:13: I will surely consume them, saith the LORD: there shall be no grapes on the vine, nor figs on the fig tree, and the leaf shall fade; and the things that I have given them shall pass away from them.

Not believing God's promises:

When you lack the strong faith to believe God's promises or doubt on them then you like many other believers can land in trouble for your unbelief.

Luk 1:12: And when Zacharias saw him, he was troubled, and fear fell upon him.

Luk 1:19: And the angel answering said unto him, I am Gabriel, that stand in the presence of God; and am sent to speak unto thee, and to shew thee these glad tidings.

Luk 1:20: And, behold, thou shalt be dumb, and not able to speak, until the day that these things shall be performed, because thou believest not my words, which shall be fulfilled in their season.

Disapproving God's blessing

God gives you a talent and you despise it, want the talent you see in some other person. If you condemn your talent and say what is the use of it to me, you are despising God and not taking God's gift with happiness. It's human courtesy to take a gift with a smile on face. If it is the order of the world to accept gifts with thankfulness how dare you reject or mock a God's given gift or priority.

Gen 25:31: And Jacob said, Sell me this day thy birthright.

Gen 25:32: And Esau said, Behold, I *am* at the point to die: and what profit shall this birthright do to me?

Gen 25:33: And Jacob said, Swear to me this day; and he sware unto him: and he sold his birthright unto Jacob.

Taking God for granted/Not hearing God's warning:

Many a times we ignore wise words from spiritual elders regarding our group of friends, business partners, and other personal matters. Many times God gives us warning through many sources regarding situations which we ignore and thereby get into trouble.

1Ki 13:33: After this thing Jeroboam returned not from his evil way, but made again of the lowest of the people priests of the high places: whosoever would, he consecrated him, and he became one of the priests of the high places.

1Ki 13:34: And this thing became sin unto the house of Jeroboam, even to cut it off, and to destroy it from off the face of the earth.

Not knowing God:

Knowing there is a God, yet not obeying the will of God.

Jer 4:22: For my people is foolish, they have not known me; they are sottish children, and they have none understanding: they are wise to do evil, but to do good they have no knowledge.

Jer 5:4: Therefore I said, Surely these are poor; they are foolish: for they know not the way of the LORD, nor the judgment of their God.

Planning by man against God's will

Most of the time man plans for self against Gods plan, the result is catastrophic; it can produce many bad situations and troubles in every walk of life, not only for the present generation but for the future generations also. The decisions made by man without God's consent can be a cause of life time agony, changing the entire course of events and the very history of the world itself. Later, only repentance and prayers can alter or control the after effects of the decision by and through God alone.

Gen 11:4: And they said, Go to, let us build us a city and a tower, whose top may reach unto heaven; and let us make us a name, lest we be scattered abroad upon the face of the whole earth.

Gen 11:8: So the LORD scattered them abroad from thence upon the face of all the earth: and they left off to build the city.

Gen 16:2: And Sarai said unto Abram, Behold now, the LORD hath restrained me from bearing: I pray thee, go in unto my maid; it may be that I may obtain children by her. And Abram hearkened to the voice of Sarai.

Gen 16:3: And Sarai Abram's wife took Hagar her maid the Egyptian, after Abram had dwelt ten years in the land of Canaan, and gave her to her husband Abram to be his wife.

Gen 16:4: And he went in unto Hagar, and she conceived: and when she saw that she had conceived, her mistress was despised in her eyes.

11

Not Giving Tithe

Holding back what is due to God from your first fruits to finance. God calls it robbing God.

Mark12:41-43: And he sat down opposite the treasury and watched the people putting money into the offering box. Many rich people put in large sums. And a poor widow came and put in two small copper coins, which make a penny. And he called his disciples to him and said to them, "Truly, I say to you, this poor widow has put in more than all those who are contributing to the offering box. For they all contributed out of their abundance, but she out of her poverty has put in everything she had, all she had to live on."

2Corin:9:1: Each one must give as he has decided in his heart, not reluctantly or under compulsion, for God loves a cheerful giver.

Malachi 3:10: Bring the full tithe into the storehouse, that there may be food in my house. And thereby put me to the test, says the Lord of hosts, if I will not open the windows of heaven for you and pour down for you a blessing until there is no more need.

The results of sin:

- Personal relation with God gets affected.
- You lose the peace of mind you had when you walked with God.
- You tend to make all the wrong decisions in your life.
- You struggle with day-to-day activities.

- Your life turns out to be a life of burden with no joy.
- You become depressed and lose hope.
- You become worldly and all your ambitions are of the world.
- Life becomes a trial.
- Diseases and pestilences affect you.
- You lack the overall peace of mind.
- When your sin is excessive, the day-to-day necessities become a struggle.
- Natural calamities can result if the entire nation or state sins.

(2Ch 6:26): When the heaven is shut up, and there is no rain, because they have sinned against thee; *yet* if they pray toward this place, and confess thy name, and turn from their sin, when thou dost afflict them.

Wars and outbreak of plagues and disease can be due to sin.

Getting widowed, losing children, barrenness are all the results of not following the entire commandments recorded in the Bible.

Apart from major sins, other matters as not thanking God for granted prayer request come under unfaithfulness to God.

Vanity and pride in self is a great sin against God.

At times, people who have been praying for a promotion highlight extra hours of hard work they put in as their reason of success and do not consider it to be the kindness of the Lord. This is why God speaks of unfaithful generation.

When you start acknowledging God in all matters great or small in your life you also start appreciating all the people who played a major role in your life and your achievements. This nature of yours to be faithful in all matters only manifests when God works in your soul and transforms you to a good individual.

Section 2

SINS AGAINST OTHERS

Introduction

This section gives a bird's eye view on the various positions and qualities each person in a family needs to possess as per biblical standards to live a harmonious life here in the Lord. Every family consists of parents, grandparents, children, aunts, uncles and cousins. The societies consist of neighbors, authorities and spiritual leaders. Bible has clearly laid out the roles each individual should have and the qualities for that role. Hence it's easy to evaluate yourself to see if you are abiding by the same. When you deviate from the commands you displease the mighty God and become a stumbling block to people around you. The sins committed against others include deviations in your behaviour towards family, Authorities/ Dignitaries and people around you.

This section highlights on the commandments to husbands and wives, children, young and old women, widows, young men and old men and all who do God's work.

The first institution formed by God in this world was family. The husband was appointed as head of the family and wife as his helpmate. The sequence of God's creation and the biblical references clearly indicates that woman shall be dominated by her husband due to her sin. Before Eve sinned they had equal rights though Eve was Adam's helpmate. But after sin entered their lives and as they were chased out from the garden of Eden, God clearly stated that as a punishment for the disobedience committed by Eve and later transferring the sin to Adam by making him eat the fruit of tree of knowledge of good and evil, Adam was to dominate Eve and she was to bear children in sorrow.

Every member of the family should love and be of support to each other and should help out each other in the family's daily routines When there is disharmony, hatred, vengeance, dislike, arguments and lack of prayer, a family merely exists by name. Bible specifies certain codes for maintenance of family, love and peace through laws and commandments. Any believer following the commandments and law of the Bible is less likely to have an unhappy family. Any disrespect to the head of the family is an insult to Christ.

Woman can suggest on important issues and decision making, but the final execution of the decision and the very decision should be left to the head of family who should be a believer fearing God. The criteria for woman to be obedient are that her husband needs to be God fearing (only a God fearing man can make the right decisions).

Any men living contrary to the Bible and its commandments better depend on their God fearing wives or elders of the house who live righteously to decide on important family matters. These rules of men holding superior position only accounts when one is a righteous man.

12

Divorcing

Before dwelling into the topic of divorce, it could be wise to know from the Bible the various commandments given to young man, old man, young woman, older women, and to the husband & wife.

Commandments to Husbands and Wives

At creation, God made the male and then the female and placed them together. Hence, What God ordained for togetherness? No man has the right to split apart, this is in regard to any married couple. If each person in the family understands their roles and duties family problems can be avoided. But when the woman takes on a man's role and vice versa, confusion sets in because God has made each of them accordingly. Every man should understand the role God has placed him in and should be humble enough to accept that role.

Marriage is a covenant you make, in front of God, and it needs to be kept holy; you should be loyal to it as God is the head. A wife should know her responsibilities and should execute them and so should the husband. Family prayers and thanksgiving should be kept regularly as an indication that this family considers God as its head. Where God is the head of the family, the family stays together.

1Co 11:3: But I would have you know, that the head of every man is Christ; and the head of the woman is the man; and the head of Christ is God.

Most of the men don't regard Christ in their lives. Such men cannot be righteous and are a burden to their families. These are men who are perverse, adulterers, covetous, evil-minded, drug addicts, drunkards etc. How can a man of no morals run a family? Hence the very point is that husbands should be God fearing with Christ as head and following the commandments of the Lord. A happy family in Christ join together and pray every morning and evening. Such families are fruitful trees whose children are responsible and later become useful adults to the world and live a good life of testimony.

Commandments to Husbands:

- Fights between husband and wife should be resolved before going to sleep or else it can hinder prayer life.
- Never to divorce unless the wife is caught in fornication.

Bible clearly indicates that no man is allowed to marry a divorced woman or take another's wife if he does so he commits adultery.

- Husbands are supposed to love their wives as Christ loved the Church. The depth of the statement is fearful as only a man committed to Christian living can ever love his wife the way Christ loved the Church (unconditional love).
- Give honour to your wife and be patient with her.

1Pe 3:7: Ye husbands, in like manner, dwell with *your wives* according to knowledge, giving honor unto the woman, as unto the weaker vessel, as being also joint-heirs of the grace of life; to the end that your prayers be not hindered.

Eph 5:25: Husbands, love your wives, even as Christ also loved the church, and gave himself up for it;

Eph 5:28: Even so ought husbands also to love their own wives as their own bodies. He that loveth his own wife loveth himself:

Eph 5:33: Nevertheless do ye also severally love each one his own wife even as himself; and *let* the wife *see* that she fear her husband.

Commandments to Wives:

- To be subject to husbands.
- Respect your husbands.
- Should be virtuous.
- Fearing God.
- Good works.
- Temperate and faithful.
- Chaste behaviour.
- Not external appearance but meek and quiet spirit.
- Husband should be proud of his wife.
- Bible says a prudent wife is from the Lord.
- Should be hard working and take care of home.

Every wife ought to be the comfort zone and helpmate for her husband. She is to maintain order, discipline at home with patience, hospitality and chaste behaviour. She should be hardworking, longsuffering; praying for the family's spiritual and other needed requirements and her husband's heart should trust her. There is no harm if a woman works to meet the family's needs but make sure the kids and husband are not totally neglected.

The women should be quiet when required to, not argumentative and submitting all matters to God in prayer. The children should be brought up in the fear of God for which the husband and wife should equally share the burden of their child to grow spiritually. Today, divorces have increased because the last generation never bothered to bring up their children in Godly love and principles and the present generation do not know how to handle family life. The woman has become a social wife of parties and fun, more than a house wife who is concerned in the proper upbringing of her children. In today's world it's stylish to be member of clubs, come late at night, attend meetings, and neglect your time with kids. You don't even know how your kid is growing up and who his/her friends are?

For a working woman it's difficult to juggle work with family responsibilities. A woman who is really concerned for her kids needs to spend time with God. Especially if kids are uncooperative the only way is to ask God to set everything straight. No man can do everything with perfection until God guides you. Most of the time, I even depend on God to wake me up. I have learned that only prayer can make you a perfect person. From small matters to great burdens, I have learned to depend on the Lord. I have found that when you have prayed for anything that troubles you, you are at peace.

God works in the other person's life to make your burden lighter and brings in lots of helpers to assist you and to take you out of the present situation. Hence don't panic if you are a child of God you can do many things without losing the balance in your life.

1Pe 3:1: In like manner, ye wives, *be* in subjection to your own husbands; that, even if any obey not the word, they may without the word be gained by the behavior of their wives;

1Pe 3:2: beholding your chaste behavior *coupled* with fear.

1Pe 3:3: Whose *adorning* let it not be the outward adorning of braiding the hair, and of wearing jewels of gold, or of putting on apparel;

1Pe 3:4: but *let it be* the hidden man of the heart, in the incorruptible *apparel* of a meek and quiet spirit, which is in the sight of God of great price.

1Pe 3:5: For after this manner aforetime the holy women also, who hoped in God, adorned themselves, being in subjection to their own husbands:

1Pe 3:6: as Sarah obeyed Abraham, calling him Lord: whose children ye now are, if ye do well, and are not put in fear by any terror.

Laws for couples:

Should not stay away from each other without another's consent.

If one amongst the husband and wife is not a believer, and if they have peace and are content to live with each other, they may continue to be together.

Do not commit adultery.

Only if the husband be dead is the wife free to marry another.

Only if the man or woman is caught in adultery should they leave each other and stay apart.

1Co 7:5: Defraud ye not one the other, except it be by consent for a season, that ye may give yourselves unto prayer, and may be together again, that Satan tempt you not because of your incontinency.

1Co 7:10: But unto the married I give charge, *yea* not I, but the Lord, That the wife depart not from her husband.

1Co 7:11: (but should she depart, let her remain unmarried, or else be reconciled to her husband); and that the husband leave not his wife.

1Co 7:12: But to the rest say I, not the Lord: If any brother hath an unbelieving wife, and she is content to dwell with him, let him not leave her.

1Co 7:13: And the woman that hath an unbelieving husband, and he is content to dwell with her, let her not leave her husband.

1Co 7:14: For the unbelieving husband is sanctified in the wife and the unbelieving wife is sanctified in the brother: else were your children unclean; but now are they holy.

Laws for men and women:

Every prayer made by a woman should be with her head covered. Uncovering the head and praying is equivalent to despising her husband and disobeying God. A woman who cannot adjust to her family can never be a pious woman.

A woman praying in public with her head uncovered disgraces God. If you do not pray the way your father in heaven has commanded you, how can your prayer be heard?

1Co 11:4: Every man praying or prophesying, having his head covered, dishonoreth his head.

1Co 11:5: But every woman praying or prophesying with her head unveiled dishonoreth her head; for it is one and the same thing as if she were shaven.

1Co 11:6: For if a woman is not veiled, let her also be shorn: but if it is a shame to a woman to be shorn or shaven, let her be veiled.

1Co 11:7: For a man indeed ought not to have his head veiled, forasmuch as he is the image and glory of God: but the woman is the glory of the man.

1Co 11:13: Judge ye in yourselves: is it seemly that a woman pray unto God unveiled?

If each of the concerned people of your family follows the commandments of the Bible, you will be part of a very happy family in the Lord.

Virtuous women:

Pro 12:4: A virtuous woman *is* a crown to her husband: but she that maketh ashamed *is* as rottenness in his bones.

Pro 18:22: *Whoso* findeth a wife findeth a good *thing*, and obtaineth favour of the LORD.

Pro 19:14: House and riches *are* the inheritance of fathers: and a prudent wife *is* from the Lord.

Pro 31:10: Who can find a virtuous woman? for her price *is* far above rubies.

Pro 31:11: The heart of her husband doth safely trust in her, so that he shall have no need of spoil.

Pro 31:30: Favour *is* deceitful, and beauty *is* vain: *but* a woman *that* feareth the LORD, she shall be praised.

Eph 5:24: But as the church is subject to Christ, so *let* the wives also *be* to their husbands in everything.

Women's qualities:

1Ti 3:11: Women in like manner *must be* grave, not slanderers, temperate, faithful in all things.

Women's attire:

1Ti 2:9: In like manner, that woman adorns themselves in modest apparel, with shamefacedness and sobriety; not with braided hair, and gold or pearls or costly raiment;

Rev 19:32: Thou shalt rise up before the hoary head, and honour the face of the old man, and fear thy God: I *am* the LORD.

Role of aged women:

Reverent in demeanor,

Not slanderers

Nor enslaved to much wine

Teachers of that which is good

Train the young women to love their husbands, to love their children

Sober-minded

Chaste

Workers at home

Kind

Being in subjection to their own husbands, that the word of God be not blasphemed.

Tit 2:3: that aged women likewise be reverent in demeanor, not slanderers nor enslaved to much wine, teachers of that which is good;

Tit 2:4: that they may train the young women to love their husbands, to love their children,

Tit 2:5: *to be* sober-minded, chaste, workers at home, kind, being in subjection to their own husbands, that the word of God be not blasphemed:

Young women:

1Pe 5:5: Likewise, ye younger, be subject unto the elder. Yea, all of you gird yourselves with humility, to serve one another: for God resisteth the proud, but giveth grace to the humble.

1Pe 5:6: Humble yourselves therefore under the mighty hand of God, that he may exalt you in due time;

Older men:

Tit 2:2: that aged men be temperate, grave, sober-minded, sound in faith, in love, in patience:

Young Man

Sober-minded

Ensample of good works; in thy doctrine

Uncorrupt

Good standing and great boldness in faith.

Tit 2:6: the younger men likewise exhort to be sober-minded:

Tit 2:7: in all things showing thyself an ensample of good works; in thy doctrine *showing* uncorruptness, gravity,

Widows:

1Ti 5:9: Let none be enrolled as a widow under threescore years old, *having been* the wife of one man,

1Ti 5:10: well reported for good works; if she hath brought up children, if she hath used hospitality to strangers, if she hath washed the saints' feet, if she hath relieved the afflicted, if she hath diligently followed every good work.

1Ti 5:11: But younger widows refuse: for when they have waxed wanton against Christ, they desire to marry;

1Ti 5:14: I desire therefore that the younger *widows* marry, bear children, rule the household, and give no occasion to the adversary for reviling.

Divorce a sin --Laws for marriage:

Over the years as a practicing dentist I came across lots of divorced people and as each year progressed the number of divorced people has increased. Out of sheer curiosity to know the exact reason I always used to have long friendly chats with them. The reasons were 75% immature and just 25% genuine. The basic problem lies in selecting partners, when Abraham wanted a wife for his son he kept Gods commandments in mind and prayerfully send his servant. Now a day's selecting partners mostly depends on financial soundness and external appearances, this is just a catastrophe. Secondly, the partners start a family life with parties and not prayers. Thirdly, they started on together for the wrong reasons and when responsibilities sets in, they just neglect their part and start living a bachelor life, this results in couples going apart. Reasons can be many; from snoring to didn't take me to movies, parties and shopping regularly, didn't help me with cooking and cleaning, is a male chauvinist, I don't want kids now he does or vice versa and the men complain that she is never at home, always visits the parents house, indifferent to my parents, flirt and the list goes on. (These are the commonest Asian side of the problems). And needless to mention the bank accounts that separates his money and her money. After marriage Bible says they are not separate but one.

Mar 10:6: But from the beginning of the creation God made them male and female.

Mar 10:7: For this cause shall a man leave his father and mother, and cleave to his wife;

Mar 10:8: And they twain shall be one flesh: so then they are no more twain, but one flesh.

Mar 10:9: What therefore God hath joined together, let not man put asunder.

Heb 13:4: *Let* marriage *be* had in honor among all, and *let* the bed *be* undefiled: for fornicators and adulterers God will judge.

Mat 5:32: But I say unto you, That whosoever shall put away his wife, saving for the cause of fornication, causeth her to commit adultery: and whosoever shall marry her that is divorced committeth adultery.

13

Disobedient to Parents

Children are a gift from God. It's the duty of every parent to bring up the child in the commandments and laws of the Bible. And Bible has given commandments on both how to bring up children and how children should be obedient to parents. Parents should instill Gods laws and commandments and teach them from young age. The teaching of Bible should be ever embossed in the child's heart not to depart from the commandments till death. Parents should daily keep their children in prayer. They should be taught to confirm that Jesus is Lord, be baptized, partake in the Lord's Table and live a righteous life. If not, it's the moral responsibility of the parents to shed tears in the presence of Lord day and night for his renewal.

Pro 17:6: Children's children *are* the crown of old men; and the glory of children *are* their fathers.

Commandment to Children:

- Respect your parents.
- Honour parents and take care of them.
- Be obedient to their advice.
- Do not revolt against them.
- Do not curse or talk back to them.

Every child born into this world is God sent. Regardless of how and where they are born they are the children of God. But once the child starts growing the parents should mould them, to be worthy in the eyes of mighty God. It is not how smart or how beautiful he or she is that matters but how well you have lived this life in the Lord which ultimately counts. If parents have spent time and energy to make them God fearing then when they grow up, they will be good and consoling otherwise, they will be a pain to the parents till their death. Only children who are God fearing can be good children.

Mat 15:4: "For God commanded, saying, Honour thy father and mother: and, He that curseth father or mother, let him die the death".

Pro 20:20: Whoso curseth his father or his mother, his lamp shall be put out in obscure darkness.

Mar 7:10: "For Moses said, Honour thy father and thy mother; and, Whoso curseth father or mother, let him die the death":

Blessing for respecting parents:

Gen 9:26: And he said, Blessed *be* the LORD God of Shem; and Canaan shall be his servant.

Lev 19:3: Ye shall fear every man his mother, and his father, and keep my sabbaths: I *am* the LORD your God.

Eph 6:1: Children, obey your parents in the Lord: for this is right.

Eph 6:2: Honor thy father and mother (which is the first commandment with promise),

Eph 6:3: that it may be well with thee, and thou mayest live long on the earth.

14

Provoking Children

Let me first introduce to the ideal parents that God had in plan and then we will have a glimpse of the present day parents.

Eph 6:4: And, ye fathers, provoke not your children to wrath: but nurture them in the chastening and admonition of the Lord.

- Children should be brought up to know and respect God.
- Children should be disciplined in commandments.
- Children should be admonished and corrected when required with firmness.
- Children should be taught to respect elders.
- Children should be taught to depend only on God.
- Should never love children above God.
- Should ceaselessly pray for them.
- Do not provoke your children to wrath.
- Nurture them in the Lord.

Don't love children above God:

1Sa 2:29: Wherefore kick ye at my sacrifice and at mine offering, which I have commanded *in my* habitation; and honourest thy sons above me, to make yourselves fat with the chiefest of all the offerings of Israel my people?

1Sa 2:31: Behold, the days come, that I will cut off thine arm, and the arm of thy father's house, that there shall not be an old man in thine house.

Children should be disciplined:

Pro 19:18: Chasten thy son while there is hope, and let not thy soul spare for his crying.

Pro 13:24: He that spareth his rod hateth his son: but he that loveth him chasteneth him betimes.

15

Not Bringing Up Children in a God-fearing Path

1Sa 8:3: And his sons walked not in his ways, but turned aside after lucre, and took bribes, and perverted judgment.

Pro 22:6: Train up a child in the way he should go: and when he is old, he will not depart from it.

Parents of present generation

In the above pages you read the instruction manual for parents as per the Bible. Now let me come to the present times and brief my readers on what is happening now days. A couple very well placed in society extremely busy with their jobs working mostly late night, decides to have a child. From the womb the child is not getting the proper nutrition, the mother feeds on all the junk foods available and finally at the end of the term a small baby is born. Mother somehow manages to be with the new born for a mere two weeks and then hurries to join back duty. This baby born into this world hardly sees his parents and only has contact with a maid or his grandma. After a year, with no counseling or love from his parents he starts to show irritability and throws tantrums. The immediate problem solver the child psychologist, child counselors, parents all sit together and discuss how to solve the problem. Meanwhile, the child starts hating his own parents who were not available with the kid when he was small. Now it is expected from him, to behave well. Some kids change because the lessons told by the child councilor is a new story which he is hearing for the first time in his life. The rest of the kids resolve to other means. By now the psychologist has classified this kids problem into Anxiety disorder, Attention deficit/Hyperactivity disorder, Disruptive behaviour, Pervasive development (confused kid), Eating disorder, Elimination disorder, Learning disorder, Affective disorder (mood changes), Schizophrenia, Tic disorder etc. Yes this is the commonest list and now this is done after recognizing symptoms which include abuse of drugs, inability to cope with problems, physical ailments, altered sleep pattern, defying authority, anger, loss of interest, loneliness, disobedience, tantrums and hallucination. After all the analysis and counseling session if child shows no change in attitude then comes the medication part. Remember one point here, till now the parents has not even kept this matter in prayer to the great physician above. And the human endeavor continues with the doctors to correct the child. Finally, it was decided to start this child on medications. To list the commonest medications they are: Antipsycotics, Antidepressants, antianxiety, stimulants and mood stabilizing drugs. I request the readers to check out the side effects of these drugs on the internet which are: antipsychotic drug takers are highly prone to diabetes and weight gain. Coming to antidepressants it warns be careful while taking these medications they can sometimes have these little adverse effects such as hallucinations, confusions, aggressions, and addiction. The reader could have had enough so I am not detailing the adverse effects possible for the rest of the drugs.

Now, as a parent you have not lived biblically, no family prayers, no guidance and you are not at home for your child and then later on you put him through all these pressures in life, it was better that this child was not born at all. Do not be parents if you don't have the time to take care of your own child, in the way the Bible instructs. If you bring forth a child without the time to care for him you will never have the peace of mind nor is your child going to be a blessing for you.

16

Not Concerned for Your Brother

Thanks to this commandment or else the present day courts and lawyers couldn't be able to handle the millions of court cases coming in on a daily basis. Family feuds, property division, financial cheating, usury all are due to the default of this commandment.

Not concerned for your brother:

How do you show concern for your brothers here are few examples?

- Do not consider your brother an enemy.
- Do not wrong your brother.
- Help your brother when your brother is in trouble.
- Help your brother financially when your brother is in need.
- Should not give money on usury to your brother.
- Never fight or argue with your brother inflicting hurt by words or deeds.
- Never fight over property matters let the elders decide what's due to you.
- Never take your brother to the judiciary; resolve the problem at home in the presence of elders.
- Never provoke your brother or spread lies about him.
- Never cheat or dishonor them.
- Never curse or be jealous of your brother.
- Pray for your brother and his protection and goodness.

Admonish as brother:

2Th 3:15: And *yet* count him not as an enemy, but admonish him as a brother.

Against brother:

4:6: that no man transgress, and wrong his brother in the matter: because the Lord is an avenger in all these things, as also we forewarned you and testified.

Concern for brother

Gen 14:14: And when Abram heard that his brother was taken captive, he armed his trained servants, born in his own house, three hundred and eighteen, and pursued them unto Dan.

Gen 14:16: And he brought back all the goods, and also brought again his brother Lot, and his goods, and the women also, and the people. (a warning from God that the place you are staying is not safe before the destruction).

Lev 25:35: And if thy brother be waxen poor, and fallen in decay with thee; then thou shalt relieve him: *yea, though he be* a stranger, or a sojourner; that he may live with thee.

Lev 25:36: Take thou no usury of him, or increase: but fear thy God; that thy brother may live with thee.

Lev 25:37: Thou shalt not give him thy money upon usury, nor lend him thy victuals for increase.

Do not be angry with your brother:

Mat 5:22: "But I say unto you, That whosoever is angry with his brother without a cause shall be in danger of the judgment: and whosoever shall say to his brother, Raca, shall be in danger of the council: but whosoever shall say, Thou fool, shall be in danger of hell fire".

The above laws are applicable to all your extended family members.

17

Misunderstandings

It is extremely common to have misunderstandings for many reasons. The commonest is relatives conveying false information to one another. Secondly, few of us are extremely sensitive to lack of concern from our siblings which is sometimes unreasonable too. Verbal arguments that keep you apart, your likings and disliking differs and problems arising from the extreme concepts and principles. Religious differences among siblings. All the above factors can lead to misgivings. It is a failure to understand your siblings correctly. You have to be accommodative and communicate well to solve this disease. Most of the cold war's are due to misunderstandings. Commonest misunderstandings occur when we speak at the wrong time, not hearing properly and understanding what was said, react differently or overreact or sometimes under react. Differences in religion, culture, race, social class and sometimes gender. How can you solve a misunderstanding? If someone who you love so much is not behaving or responding in the same way as before you can assume that something has gone wrong. Now, instead of keeping a cold face and thinking I will also repay him the same way it is our moral obligation to enquire what the wrong that you have done is. If required you need to apologize also. Any behaviour that is abnormal in a person you know very well for so many years should be clarified. Sometimes individuals may not smile back at you or ignore you, or look through you, they might be going through tremendous pressure in some aspect and is absent minded or for all you know forgot their spectacles.

A person going through some form of trauma can ignore you because he or she is in no mood to talk and wants to be left alone. You as a Christian should be understanding, forgiving, going that extra mile to make someone happy, communicative and above all praying for the situation to pass.

Matt 5:22-25: which says "But I say unto you, that whosoever is angry with his brother without a cause shall be in danger of the judgment:

18

Unresolved Fights Within the Family

Many families hold generational grudges against each other transmitting it to the coming generation by conveying the old stories. If three generations back, two brothers had a problem then it wouldn't be wise to torment the present generation with those old stories. I remember an incident where two of the third generation of two warring families came to the same university, got admitted for the same course and were classmates. Both their families gave them strict orders of not talking to each other or even cross each other's path. Two years went on this way. Finally a highly spirited team leader asked them separately what is the problem. To his surprise he found out that it was a generational warring family problem. Somehow he resolved it, he was a social worker and he individually visited both the families on the pretext of friendship. Stayed with each of the families and made programs in college in such a way that the two students were actively participating and their parents were called to watch these programs and finally at the end of five years he managed to patch up both the families. He was a great man.

James 4:1 to 2: What causes quarrels and what causes fights among you? Is it not this that your passions are at war within you? You desire and do not have, so you murder. You covet and cannot obtain, so you fight and quarrel. You do not have, because you do not ask.

Rom 12:17-21: Repay no one evil for evil, but give thought to do what is honorable in the sight of all. If possible, so far as it depends on you, live peaceably with all. Beloved, never avenge yourselves, but leave it to the wrath of God, for it is written, "Vengeance is mine, I will repay, says the Lord." To the contrary, "if your enemy is hungry, feed him; if he is thirsty, give him something to drink; for by so doing you will heap burning coals on his head." Do not be overcome by evil, but overcome evil with good.

19

Mismanaging Finances

Many families have dropped from riches to rags. If one weak link in the family misuse the finance of the family, the entire family suffers. When you are in charge of a joint family account or nuclear family account or the family estate business the entire family is depended on you for survival. Hence, it is your moral responsibility not to spend the family income in any of your vices or pleasures at the family's expense. If you do that then your children can become vagabonds, your wife can land up in prostitution and the entire family will have to beg for the very living, your house can get sold and all of a sudden you lose all the finance you had. It is a great sin to be irresponsible towards your family.

I have seen many rich families collapse due to extravagant living and their children work in their maids houses, What a pitiable state that is.

Luke 15:13: "And not many days later, the younger son gathered everything together and went on a journey into a distant country, and there he squandered his estate with loose living."

Proverbs 29:3: A man who loves wisdom makes his father glad, but he who keeps company with harlots wastes his wealth.

20

Property Fights

Today the maximum court cases are on property issues between siblings or husband and wife. What I have understood is that every elder in the house should be wise enough to divide an equal share to his children when alive and write a will to the property. If the parents are wise enough to do all things righteously the sibling conflicts can be avoided to a large extend. One sibling will be greedier than the other in that case all the matters in a believers house hold should be settled only by the elders and not by the worldly court.

1Cor 6:1-20: When one of you has a grievance against another, does he dare go to law before the unrighteous instead of the saints? Or do you not know that the saints will judge the world? And if the world is to be judged by you, are you incompetent to try trivial cases? Do you not know that we are to judge angels? How much more, then, matters pertaining to this life! So if you have such cases, Can it be that there is no one among you wise enough to settle a dispute between the brothers.

1Cor 6:6-7: But brother goes to law against brother, and that before unbelievers? To have lawsuits at all with one another is already a defeat for you. Why not rather suffer wrong? Why not rather be defrauded?

21

Questioning Authorities

Any person holding a higher position, older than you or younger than you is to be respected. Any authorities, dignitaries, people who are your superiors should be respected regardless of what type of people they are. Always be subject to people in charge of you without rebellion says the Bible. It's human nature to forget the past and strut on the present position. Before you reach this level, think of the umpteenth number of people who played a role in your life to make you what you are today. The many masters who taught you your basic lessons and now after many years you think these masters as outdated. What a grievous sin? Bible repeatedly warns that no man can be better than his master. Every individual in this world who has played a role to build you up needs to be respected. (That includes your kinder garden teacher too)

Sins in this category can be verbal as talking bad about the institution you are working with or creating trouble for your institution, spreading false rumours, not content with your wages, breaking of laws and regulations of the institution. These also include not paying the government taxes, fighting and using harsh words against dignitaries, backbiting, bringing financial loss to the institution due to your sluggish ways, arguments, not concerned about your subordinates and juniors who refuse to work under you which can bring in financial loss to the institution.

Questioning:

A good Christian should never aim or fight for certain positions. If you are eligible for any higher positions, your loving colleagues or your management will place you there. Questioning authorities why you were not put in a higher position is sin in the eyes of our Lord. You need not fight for positions or powers or manipulate to get there. You should be faithful to the institution you work for and do your job with all your might. You, as a good Christian should be concerned about the institutions perfect functioning and for the wellbeing of all your juniors and colleagues working there than your higher post. You should only think on terms of bringing gains and good name to your institution.

If you are unhappy with your present job, look for different job options and move out with decency instead of creating a scene there. If you are not happy with your wages do not keep finding fault with management, you ask them for a hike and if you deserve it then you will get or else find a new job. Be hardworking, organized and disciplined as good role models in the institution you work for. Be a peace maker, reliable, whom others can depend on, whose presence bring happiness and thought of respect in the minds of others. You, as a good Christian should be the pride and pillar of the institution you work for.

22

Abusing Authorities

Misusing or misemploying the office for illegal or personal gains. Many times the official post or office is misused by diverting funds for personal gains, illegally permitting outsiders access to the office computers to take out information's pertaining to the office or employers. Helping an opponent company by giving confidential information's. In total, anything that can cause a financial loss to the institution or bad reputation to the institution is an abuse.

In short:

- Should not disobey their commands in job matters.
- Should not mock them or tease them.
- Should not murmur or complaint against them.
- Should not back stab them or abuse them.
- Should not criticize them or be unfaithful towards them.
- No man is greater than his master.
- Complete the work assigned to you at the said time.
- Do a hundred percent complete hearted job.
- Do not think that your decisions are better than the decisions made by your superiors.
- Should not ridicule authorities.
- Spoiling the harmony among the subordinates is wrong.
- Not able to work congenially with colleagues is also wrong.

23

Threatening Authorities

We should not scold or threaten our authorities. Threatening is not only verbal abuse but can be in various forms. For example, after years of expertise in your field you become the very soul of your institution and is the key person in the smooth functioning of your office matters and the authorities look up to you for everything. When you are offered a higher pay by a new company and if you leave your old institution without prior notice or without training someone else to substitute you then it becomes a sin as you did not give sufficient time for the authorities to find a good substitute. Some officers are indispensible to an institution and their sudden absence can cause great loss to the institution and this is one form of threat to the authorities. Another form of threat is when you know you are indispensible and you start taking advantage of this situation, by asking for a hike in your salary every now and then with the threatening note that you are going to leave. This is a great sin as per the biblical teaching. Bible says be content with your wages. Bible insist that we should not mock people, we should not use bad language against officers holding higher post and against our authorities.

Man needs to respect every individual. He can certainly advice or show them the right path with patience and long suffering.

Exo 22:28: Thou shalt not revile the Gods, nor curse the ruler of thy people.

2Pe 2:10: but chiefly them that walk after the flesh in the lust of defilement, and despise dominion. Daring, self-willed, they tremble not to rail at dignities:

2Pe 2:11: whereas angels, though greater in might and power, bring not a railing judgment against them before the Lord.

24

Causing Factions/Divisions

This commonly happens in an institution which is named as playing politics and causing division amongst brethren/colleagues. This can happen in a congregation, institution or a country. God hates strife creating people and expects us to respect and honour all. Causing division in working environment harming everyone around you is dangerous because you are going to fall into the same trap.

1Pe 2:17: Honor all men. Love the brotherhood. Fear God. Honor the king.

Heb 13:17: Obey them that have the rule over you, and submit *to them*: for they watch in behalf of your souls, as they that shall give account; that they may do this with joy, and not with grief: for this *were* unprofitable for you.

Rom 13:1-2: Let every soul be subject unto the higher powers. For there is no power but of God: the powers that be are ordained of God.

Whosoever therefore resisteth the power resisteth the ordinance of God. This can be by causing trouble or tale bearing or any method in short if you are the reason for a conflict you will be judged.

Commandments for masters/servants

God only seeks and requires that masters be kind, giving, and of an understanding heart. Treat your servants, as you wished your heavenly father to treat you. Don't hold their wages or tax them excessively. Don't threaten people who work for you.

Col 4:1: Masters, render unto your servants that which is just and equal; knowing that ye also have a Master in heaven.

Eph 6:9: And, ye masters, do the same things unto them, and forbear threatening: knowing that he who is both their Master and yours is in heaven, and there is no respect of persons with him.

Commandments to Servants

A servant needs to be accountable, faithful, and loyal in all aspects to the master; God has commanded the servants to do all work as if they were doing it for God. Servants are also admonished to be well pleasing, not complaining, and to tolerate the master in all aspects within the will of God.

Tit 2:9: *Exhort* servants to be in subjection to their own masters, *and* to be well-pleasing *to them* in all things; not gainsaying.

Tit 2:10: not purloining, but showing all good fidelity; that they may adorn the doctrine of God our Saviour in all things.

1Pe 2:18: Servants, *be* in subjection to your masters with all fear; not only to the good and gentle, but also to the froward.

1Pe 2:19: For this is acceptable, if for conscience toward God a man endureth griefs, suffering wrongfully.

Eph 6:5: Servants, be obedient unto them that according to the flesh are your masters, with fear and trembling, in singleness of your heart, as unto Christ.

Eph 6:6: not in the way of eye service, as men-pleasers; but as servants of Christ, doing the will of God from the heart.

Eph 6:7: with good will doing service, as unto the Lord, and not unto men.

Eph 6:8: knowing that whatsoever good thing each one doeth, the same shall he receive again from the Lord, whether *he be* bond or free.

The most beautiful aspect of the above verse is that if you are sincere in all matters to your institution or to your superiors and has done all the work asked by them to your full effort, our mighty God tells us even if they don't understand your effort or give you a salary hike or consider your goodwill, your heavenly father has taken note of all matters and is going to reward you. What a wonderful promise and privilege. By how you live your life here God is going to give you responsible positions in heaven.

25

Talebearing

Most of the sins by words are via speech, advice, anger, and arguments. Complaints, murmuring, putting down others, rebuking elders in a provocative manner, answering back and boasting are sins in regard to speech. Corrupt speech proceeds out of man due to lack of fear of God. Any man that fears God will think twice before talking. The cause of loose tongue is that man has moved away from God. When that happens he imagines evil and from his thoughts precede all corrupt ungodly speech. A good Christian uses his tongue wisely.

Tale-Bearing:

All sorts of rumors, exaggerated truths are all transmitted by these agents called tale bearers. God commanded man to do all things that are of benefit or purpose and for use to mankind. Any activity that's of no use to any one is a sin. In fact, these sins hurt others and kill your soul. If these facts you collect about others are of no use to anyone, it is better to refrain from collecting information and passing it on. People have a tendency to talk wrong things, criticize others, ridicule and use harsh foul words on others provoking them to respond angrily. A good Christian uses only words of wisdom as encouragement, advice, counseling or words of peace. Bible says that peacemakers shall surely inherit the kingdom of God. As a child of God it's your responsibility not to add fuel to the fire by your words.

Pro 11:13: A talebearer revealeth secrets: but he that is of a faithful spirit concealeth the matter.

Pro 18:8: The words of a talebearer *are* as wounds, and they go down into the innermost parts of the belly.

Jas 3:6: And the tongue is a fire: the world of iniquity among our members is the tongue, which defileth the whole body, and setteth on fire the wheel of nature, and is set on fire by hell.

26

False Witness/Swear Falsely

Never swear on anything or anyone. God says that if you cannot make a hair black or grey than why you need to swear by it. Let all your words be yes or no. Perjurer is a person giving false testimony. This is a great sin because you are putting an innocent man behind bars with your false statement. In many criminal cases, people are influenced or paid hefty sums to give false testimony. If this could happen to Jesus Christ then what about each of us. As Christians many times false testimony by others can get us into trouble, the only way is to pray for the perjurer that God one day touch his heart and he may live a free man. I have seen many Christians stand as false witness for hefty sums. Never ever do it as you will not benefit from this gift of money in turn you might need to spend thousands in hospital for various diseases and accidents resulting from sin.

Jer 7:9: Will ye steal, murder, and commit adultery, and swear falsely, and burn incense unto Baal, and walk after other Gods whom ye know not;

1Pe 3:10: For, He that would love life, And see good days, Let him refrain his tongue from evil, And his lips that they speak no guile:

27

Mocking/Teasing

A mocker jeers or mocks or treats something with contempt or calls out in derision. A mutterer or complainer, can be a person who grumbles for any responsibility given to him. He/She detest responsibility and hate to have guest at home. Many times we murmur when our work load is in excess or when we need to work overtime. Consider the overall benefit of working overtime, if you're working overtime benefits someone in a good way, keep it in the hands of Lord and pray to God to give you the energy to complete the work. If it's normal household chores or taking care of surprise guests or its regarding your work or studies, do your part and place the burden on Christ. God knows how much you can take and also knows how to take you through the present situation.

If you hear something which you do not like and start complaining or grumbling without asking the will of God, you lose your testimony with God and man. Every burden in your heart, every desire in your heart, should be what God wants in your life. If you desire, only the will of God in your life, all that comes your way is dealt with by God. Throughout the Bible you see one thing: God hates complainers and murmurers because they ask and desire things contrary to God or loudly complain before even asking God, what is the present situation.

People complain of work overload while all you need to do is ask for God's grace to give you the strength to complete it. People complain of visitors coming home, ask God's grace to treat them with utmost respect. Be hospitable and kind because in olden days Bible says many have entertained angels unawares.

Do not murmur or complain against any situation, see what you can achieve by prayer, to overcome the situation with victory. Never find fault with others or blame others for the particular situation you are in. If you do so you are a sinner. I have seen people who blame others for everything that happens in their life.

1Co 10:10: Neither murmur ye, as some of them murmured, and perished by the destroyer.

Jas 3:9: Therewith bless we the Lord and Father; and therewith curse we men, who are made after the likeness of God:

Jas 3:10: out of the same mouth cometh forth blessing and cursing. My brethren, these things ought not so to be.

28

Misleading

We as Christians should not mislead others, if you are asked on some topic that you don't know then admit that you have no idea about it and refer to someone who'll be able to help. Many of us claim tall things and easily mislead others by stating authority over that subject. Hence, be careful to advice someone on a topic you are scarcely aware of or while transfering incorrect information from hearsays. The first example in the Bible is how Satan mislead Eve to eat the fruit and also give it to Adam. Next is misleading other by false prophecy.

Types of misleading:

- Wrong advice
- Referring to incompetent people
- Transferring hearsays
- False information
- Exaggerated information
- Half truth
- White lies
- Canvassing for personal gains
- Wrong interpretation
- Claiming authority

Jeremiah 14:14: Prophets prophesied lies in God's name. He had not sent them, commanded them, nor spoken to them, but they prophesied a false vision and the deceit of their heart.

2 Corinthian 11:13-15: "False apostles" are called "deceitful workers," because they pretend to be servants of Christ, angels of light, and ministers of righteousness.

29

Anger

Many sins stem forth from anger. Anger should be controlled at a young age. I have met many people who lost their career, friends, families, positions and opportunities due to anger. Many people in jail have committed crimes when they were angry but inconsolable as they lost their wife or children to anger. Anger is a sin that's like a slow killing poison. It kills the soul while giving way to evil. You lose all peace in your life because of anger. An angry person should introspect to Why he or she gets irritated, angry, frustrated and later depressed? Prayer is a perfect medicine to calm a person down.

Doing good things, taking time off from hectic schedules of work, music, spending time with family, doing exercise, gardening walking in the morning and meditation, quiet time with the Lord are all things that relaxes you. When someone provokes you just keep praying for that person or think of how you can improve things. Bible tells that you can be angry for good reasons which can improve things but the anger should not be permanent in the mind of the person. Bible calls an angry person foolish; people who are calm and less angry are of good understanding. Bible recommends not to be friend of an angry person.

The quoted verses from Bible are:

Rom 2:8: But unto them that are contentious, and do not obey the truth, but obey unrighteousness, indignation and wrath,

Eph 4:26: Be ye angry, and sin not: let not the sun goes down upon your wrath:

4:27: neither give place to the devil.

14:17 : *He that is* soon angry dealeth foolishly: and a man of wicked devices is hated.

Pro 14:29: *He that is* slow to wrath *is* of great understanding: but *he that is* hasty of spirit exalteth folly.

Pro 15:1: A soft answer turneth away wrath: but grievous words stir up anger.

Pro 15:18: A wrathful man stirreth up strife: but *he that is* slow to anger appeaseth strife.

Pro 22:24: Make no friendship with an angry man; and with a furious man thou shalt not go.

Pro 22:25: Lest thou learn his ways, and get a snare to thy soul.

Pro 25:23: The north wind driveth away rain: so *doth* an angry countenance a backbiting tongue.

Eph 4:31: Let all bitterness, and wrath, and anger, and clamor, and railing, be put away from you, with all malice.

30

Busy Bodies

These are people who are always bothered in finding the wrong things about others. They are named as meddling or prying people. They are busy discussing about other people's affairs or matters without correcting their own mistakes. Now this concept has two aspects, when Bible is preached to some people they are falsely accused of being busy bodies for telling the truth. But, the busy body the Bible refers to is, about a person causing trouble for others by discussing their personal matters in public. If asked to comment on an issue do it with courage, it is your opinion and you are not forcing any one to follow it. If not, leave the matter until you are asked for an opinion or to make a decision for a governing body. For Christians, Bible is the standard reference book and correction with love is permitted. All the truth is in black and white hence the reader can chose which path to take; the path of the world or the heavenly truth. From Biblical findings a busy body is one that harms a righteous man reputation.

Identifying busy bodies:

They ask about your problems, pester you till you tell them.

They discuss others matters with you and complain about them.

They are self- righteous.

They look as if they are concerned but are worse than poison.

Beware of any person, who discusses other's matters, or complain about others or criticize or curse others. Keep a distance from such kind of people and never entertain them.

2Th 3:11 For we hear of some that walk among you disorderly, that work not at all, but are busybodies.

2Th 3:12: Now them that are such we command and exhort in the Lord Jesus Christ, that with quietness they work, and eat their own bread.

2Th 3:13: But ye, brethren, be not weary in well-doing.

31

Envy/Jealousy

Envy is a feeling of discontented or resentful longing, aroused by someone else possessions, qualities, luck, or their achievements or advantages. Boasting is talking with excessive pride and self-satisfaction about one's achievements, possessions, or abilities. Now, these two are linked in such a way that generally, a boasting tongue initiates envy/jealousy. Unless, you elaborate your achievements, possessions to others in some form you cannot be envied. Hence, as Christians we need to keep a low profile or else we will be initiating sin in another person. Your boasting can cause depression, uselessness and internal conflict in others, if they are weak minded. Boasting is a sign of pride which utters words of arrogance, and unkindness without any understanding. Pride can make you overconfident, selfish and egoistic at the expense of another person's downfall.

We need to always be humble and think of all the unfortunates & orphans, how God has placed us in a better position. Bible has record of kings that became beggars and beggars that became rich man. It's the grace of God that upholds us and not our own credits. Just a movement of pride in our minds against God can put us to shame. Always be exceedingly fearful in all matters and especially of what you speak because your father in heaven is watching you. Do not grieve the Holy Spirit by your words. Every word that we speak in this world is accounted before our father unless we ask forgiveness for the same.

1Sa 2:3: Talk no more so exceeding proudly; let *not* arrogancy come out of your mouth: for the LORD *is* a God of knowledge, and by him actions are weighed.

Gal 5:26: Let us not become vainglorious, provoking one another, envying one another.

Be courteous, humble and ask God for wisdom. Solomon asked God for wisdom he was granted wisdom. If God is the one who gives us the talents what right has man to be proud of them?

Pro 25:14: Whoso boasteth himself of a false gift *is like* clouds and wind without rain.

Pro 27:1: Boast not thyself of tomorrow; for thou knowest not what a day may bring forth.

Pro 27:2: Let another man praise thee, and not thine own mouth; a stranger, and not thine own lips.

32

Troublemakers

If you visit a factory and talk to some union leaders you will soon find that some people fight for a righteous cause yet few of them fight and argue for petty matters. These people are called trouble makers. They mobilize an ignorant crowd by giving them false information about a situation and disrupt the normal functioning of an institution/factory/organization. Agitating against higher authority by force is not good, if you have a genuine reason to complain then let two or three amongst you meet the concerned authorities and make a peaceful request. Always peaceful negotiations are better than retaliation. It is in human nature to exhibit strength by using force or violent demonstrations. Many years back a violent mob burned a bus, killing down all the passengers within. As Christians we need to tackle situation peacefully because it is written in the Bible that blessed are the peace makers. Trouble makers are the main cause for religious clashes, outbreak of wars and misuse of science to destroy humanity. They are thorn in your flesh.

Corrupt speech includes jesting at another man, mocking him in his absence, belittling people to others, not giving due respect to elders in your speech are all matters of concern for your soul. God has made you and others in his own image and glory, then how can you question and ridicule the maker himself? Do you expect everyone to be like you in relation to beauty, brains, and wealth? You are mistaken, for God has made every human with a purpose in many different kinds of moulds just like how he has made some fishes ornamental, some consumable and some wild. When you construct a house you don't make all of the rooms as bathrooms or bedrooms. Each room is made to suit separate purposes according to your needs. No man has been given the right to criticize another or judge another or jest or tease another, we have only the power to correct an earring brother with affection and love.

Eph 4:29 Let no corrupt speech proceed out of your mouth, but such as is good for edifying as the need may be, that it may give grace to them that hear.

Jas 3:8: But the tongue can no man tame; *it is* a restless evil, *it is* full of deadly poison.

Pro 15:28: The heart of the righteous studieth to answer: but the mouth of the wicked poureth out evil things.

Tit 1:10: For there are many unruly men, vain talkers and deceivers, specially they of the circumcision

Tit 1:11: whose mouths must be stopped; men who overthrow whole houses, teaching things which they ought not, for filthy lucre's sake.

33

Speaking Against God's Anointed

When God has anointed someone for a purpose, no other man can judge him or criticize him. It's always better to leave God's anointed or appointed children's sin, into the hands of God itself. I have seen many assemblies split into two, because the believers are not happy with their elders or pastors or priests. Any person who is ordained to be a deacon or priest needs to first analyze themselves whether they are eligible for that post, as per the commandments (refer to the chapter on commandments for Gods workers). If so, they should be unanimously elected for the same, by the guidance of the Holy Spirit. Once elected by the guidance of Holy Spirit they needs to maintain the spiritual life as recommended by God; if not then God will remove the person from the post he holds.

Every position given by God is to be accounted for. If an owner appoints you as a caretaker for a specific purpose, he has the right to know what you are doing and how well you are doing it in that post. The same way, father in heaven expects his children to be accountable. But now comes another employee who keeps on harping about your faults and misbehavior. The owner could do two things. One, he may keep observing the caretaker more closely and if he is faultless, he should be angry with the person who complained and brand him a gossiper. If by chance all the complaints of the employee against the caretaker are true then the employer should remove the care taker from that position but never make the employee a caretaker as his nature is complaining type. Every human is smart to understand those people who are complainers, criticizers, striving for post. These people are generally not given positions because they complain and criticize. So the father in heaven also keeps the critics away.

Num 12:1: And Miriam and Aaron spake against Moses because of the Ethiopian woman whom he had married: for he had married an Ethiopian woman.

Num12:8: With him will I speak mouth to mouth, even apparently, and not in dark speeches; and the similitude of the LORD shall he behold: wherefore then were ye not afraid to speak against my servant Moses?

Num 12:9: And the anger of the LORD was kindled against them; and he departed.

Num 12:10: And the cloud departed from off the tabernacle; and, behold, Miriam *became* leprous, *white* as snow: and Aaron looked upon Miriam, and, behold, *she was* leprous.

So the golden rule says leave alone Gods servants to God to judge and do not take that burden upon you because you will be punished by God for judging his servants.

34

Unnecessary Arguments

Arguments start with your ideological differences, philosophical differences, political difference, and differences of opinion regarding family matters in relation to job and other areas of life. Once, I was searching the net and found that the most argument prone topics are: abortion is legal or not, animal right and experimentation, Breast cancer and the effects of chemicals in soaps, deodorants, ethnic adoption, plastic surgery, genetic cloning, pharmaceutical industry, human trafficking, and now-a-days beauty pageants.

Bible clearly states that difference of opinion should not result in anger or vindictive thoughts. Healthy conversation ending with peace is the protocol. No speech should end with hurt or fights. Answer argumentative questions peacefully. Let not the words of an adversary provoke you to speak rudely but speak with calmness and serenity. Only a man who prays incessantly will have the grace to answer wisely because the fear of God is beginning of wisdom. Many a times I have seen adults arguing in public using foul language.

1Pe 3:15: but sanctify in your hearts Christ as Lord: *being* ready always to give answer to every man that asketh you a reason concerning the hope that is in you, yet with meekness and fear:

Pro 26:4: Answer not a fool according to his folly, lest thou also be like unto him.

Pro 26:5: Answer a fool according to his folly, lest he be wise in his own conceit.

1Ti 1:4: neither to give heed to fables and endless genealogies, which minister questionings, rather than a dispensation of God which is in faith; *so do I now.*

1Ti 1:6: from which things some having swerved have turned aside unto vain talking;

1Ti 1:7: desiring to be teachers of the law, though they understand neither what they say, nor whereof they confidently affirm.

It need not be that you will win all arguments even if you are speaking the truth. When you know that the person you are talking to is unreasonable in understanding the concepts from your point of view and still firmly holding on to his point by raising his voice Bible says agree to your adversary not by you giving in mentally but letting him talk his feelings out.

Mat 5:25: Agree with thine adversary quickly, whiles thou art in the way with him; lest at any time the adversary deliver thee to the judge, and the judge deliver thee to the officer, and thou be cast into prison.

Ask God for the wisdom to speak and understanding to know the heart of a person. Ask God the ability to convey messages in the most cordial peaceful manner and ask God the wisdom to learn all matters. Whatever you ask for good and in the name of Jesus with faith it shall be granted unto you.

Isa 50:4: The Lord GOD hath given me the tongue of the learned, that I should know how to speak a word in season to *him that is* weary: he wakeneth morning by morning, he wakeneth mine ear to hear as the learned.

Every question should be answered with understanding and peace. A good man fears God and he speaks righteousness and as he follows Godly commandments his speech is comely and good.

1Pe 3:15: but sanctify in your hearts Christ as Lord: *being* ready always to give answer to every man that asketh you a reason concerning the hope that is in you, yet with meekness and fear:

1Pe 3:16: having a good conscience; that, wherein ye are spoken against, they may be put to shame who revile your good manner of life in Christ.

To conclude God says that a man needs to be quiet, perceive everything around him and speak only when required to do so.

1Th 4:11: and that ye study to be quiet, and to do your own business, and to work with your hands, even as we charged you;

1Th 4:12: that ye may walk becomingly toward them that are without, and may have need of nothing.

35

Strange Teachings/Doctrines

Any doctrinal advice or teaching, contrary to the Biblical commandments is a sin against God and man. Every doctrine taught should be of sound knowledge and not hearsays. Every person teaching the commandments and doctrines, should do so with Bible references and not otherwise and every person listening to it should read the Bible and confirm on the doctrine taught. What is this strange doctrine? Anything contrary to the doctrine of Christ. We follow Christ and not a particular denomination. We follow the principles from the Bible not rules framed out by elders or pastors. We believe in trinity and resurrection because the Bible states so. How each of the trinity is interrelated can cause many arguments but for sure there is a heavenly father, a son who died for us and the Holy Spirit our comforter. Who is greatest? Is Jesus only a prophet? Theories of evolution? Jesus died but did not resurrect? Was Jesus married? All these argumentative questions, theologians try to answer and counter answer, but we know for sure, we are worshipping a living God who is able to care for, hear us and protect us. Above all, we are all in a race to eternal life. Hence, do not lose your peace of mind or faith over theologically different issues or denominational doctrines. Anything that burdens your mind and heart beyond which you cannot grasp is vain and not from the Bible.

Heb 13:9: Be not carried away by divers and strange teachings: for it is good that the heart be established by grace; not by meats, wherein they that occupied themselves were not profited.

John 7:16 -18: "My teaching in not Mine, but His who sent Me". If anyone is willing to do His will, he will know of the teaching whether it is of God or whether I speak from myself. He who speaks from himself seeks his own glory;

What more proof you need?

36

Biological Warfare

Sins by action can be any harm physically done to a person or actions of yours that hurt or make a person helpless and lost. Actions can be of two types: the first one, in which you don't care for a person's feeling and do not understand his situation and taxing him to work for you. Your heart becomes cold to his feelings, problems and you are just bothered about self. This makes him bitter towards you and makes him think why he has been loyal towards you all this while. The second type of action is purposeful. You are all out to destroy that person financially, ruin his peace of mind and spoil him totally. This can be due to jealousy, vengeance on a precedent incident or rivalry (familial or otherwise).

Whatever may be the cause, you are going against the second biggest commandment of God "Love thy neighbor as thyself".

Biological Warfare:

Man destroying; incapacitating or killing; an individual, a communityoranentirenation.Ifanindividual'smurderisconsidered as a great sin then how much more sinful it is to wipe out an entire community or nation. Biological warfare, is also referred as Germ fare as it involves the use of toxins, bacteria, virus and fungi. The bioagents used to destroy are organisms, considered not to be alive in present universally but when activated can reproduce in their host. (Small pox, pneumonic plague, anthrax etc). Entomological, or insect, warfare is also a biological weapon where people use an infected insect to attack their enemy. (Bee/wasp). In the present times, many countries possess anti agriculture and anti livestock weapons to eliminate the food and animals generated by that country. Nothing can be more cruel than killing people by causing intentional famine this act cannot be called anything else except self destruction of human race. When countries can kill communities like individuals, like terrorists then why people committing crime against others are punished? What hypocrisy? "It is forbidden to kill; therefore all murderers are punished unless they kill in large numbers and to the sound of trumpets." Said Votaire how true! Let me quote Einstein here "I know not with what weapons World War III will be fought, but World War IV will be fought with sticks and stones." I wonder if that also will be left the way humans are erasing all aspects of life unless it rains sticks and stones. As Herbert Hoover stated the old wise men decide on retaliation but it is the young who die and finally Ernest Hemingway says that "Never think that war, no matter how necessary, nor how justified, is not a crime." These are words from the wise what does Bible say:

2 Corinthians 10:3-5: For though we walk in the flesh, we do not war according to the flesh, for the weapons of our warfare are not of the flesh, but divinely powerful for the destruction of fortresses. We are destroying speculations and every lofty thing raised up against the knowledge of God, and we are taking every thought captive to the obedience of Christ,

1 Chronicles 5:20: And they were helped against them, and the Hagrites and all who were with them were given into their hand; for they cried out to God in the battle, and He was entreated for them, because they trusted in Him.

John 16:33: "These things I have spoken to you, that in me you may have peace. In the world you have tribulation, but take courage; I have overcome the world."

Whatever happens trust in God, pray for your country and nations. Pray that God give us good administrators that are pleasing to our mighty God so that the decisions they make are Godly and God will go with them to protect the area they are in charge. Hence the need of the hour is to pray for Godly children to hold important positions and we as true Christians should only vote for Godly people so that we also don't face the music along with other troubled nations. From the reading of scripture we understand that if the head is a Godly person as Joshua was God will go with him.

Psalm 144:1-2: Blessed be the LORD, my rock, Who trains my hands for war, And my fingers for battle; My loving kindness and my fortress, My stronghold and my deliverer; My shield and He in whom I take refuge; Who subdues my people under me.

37

Intentional Torts

Sadistic people derives pleasure from inflicting pain, suffering, or humiliating as, they like to see others suffer the same suffering they are undergoing. Many AIDS people or people having sexually transmitted diseases, intentionally transfer this disease to their innocent wife or others without their knowledge. Intentional torts include assault, battery (touching without permission) and forceful confinement. Taking pictures while someone is bathing and putting it in the internet, defamation, neglecting duty of a teacher to protect the children during school hours etc. In general these people wants to see others in agony and they use violence, aggression and inflict pain and fear in others.

Cannibalism/eating children is a type of sadism and in some instance hardness of heart as stated in Bible and ye shall eat the flesh of your sons, and the flesh of your daughters shall ye eat. (Leviticus 26:29) and thou shalt eat the fruit of thine own body, the flesh of thy sons and of thy daughters. (Deuteronomy 28:53)

Many of the Gods prophets were beheaded, burned alive, stoned to death, put in gallows, but as Christians we need to depend and trust in God to mete out punishment and we are not to avenge anyone.(Jesus, Paul and Silas (Acts 16), the prophet Jeremiah (Jer:20:2;38:6) Vengeance belongs only to the Lord (Psalm 94:1).

38

Passive Smoking

When you smoke you emit poison into the environment and all who breathe it suffers allergies, respiratory problems and lung disease. It is a sin to cause harm to other people's health. Smoking pregnant mothers are hard hearted, with no concern for the health of the unborn. Many scientific studies have proved that continuous exposure to smoking can cause sudden infant death syndrome, asthma, bronchitis, tuberculosis, impaired respiratory function, Crohn's disease, developmental delays, and risk of middle ear infections. You are not only killing yourself but in the process you are also slowly annihilating people around you.

Why do people smoke? The reasons can be to relax, to release mental pressure, as a fad, because peers do it, because it is a cool thing whatever may be the reason. But once you are addicted to smoking it is difficult to quit.

This body is a holy temple belonging to God any misuse to the body will be judged.

1 Corinthians 6:19-20: "Don't you realize that your body is the temple of the Holy Spirit, who lives in you and was given to you by God? You do not belong to yourself, for God bought you with a high price. So you must honor God with your body."

Romans 12:2: "Don't copy the behavior and customs of this world, but let God transform you into a new person by changing the way you think. Then you will learn to know God's will for you, which is good and pleasing and perfect."

"I beseech you therefore, brethren, by the mercies of God, that ye present your bodies a living sacrifice, holy, acceptable unto God, which is your reasonable service. And be not conformed to this world: but be ye transformed by the renewing of your mind, that ye may prove what is that good, and acceptable, and perfect, will of God". (Rom. 12:1-2)

39

Unkind

What does this mean? Unkind means you are uncharitable, unpleasant, nasty, mean, disagreeable, cruel, spiteful, malicious, callous, not understanding, unsympathetic, uncaring, hurtful, cold hearted, ill natured, unruly and above all vindictive. On the other hand, Unjust implies partial, not fair, prejudiced etc.

Unfair:

If you do not pay your servants wages or if you oppress the widows and fatherless then God said that judgment is for sure. If you put stumbling block in the way of deaf, blind or the dumb God's judgment is sure. In all your dealings with others, God has commanded that, treat them as you wish to be treated. In all your dealings with your workers and subordinates you should be understanding and kind.

Mal 3:5: And I will come near to you to judgment; and I will be a swift witness against the sorcerers, and against the adulterers, and against false swearers, and against those that oppress the hireling in *his* wages, the widow, and the fatherless, and that turn aside the stranger *from his right,* and fear not me, saith the LORD of hosts.

Do Not Afflict Orphans and Widows:

The mighty God has always cared for widows and orphans. We are also commanded to care for them and if we do that then special blessings shall be bestowed on our present life and the coming one.

Exo 22:22: Ye shall not afflict any widow, or fatherless child.

Exo 22:23: If thou afflict them in any wise, and they cry at all unto me, I will surely hear their cry.

Psa 94:6: They slay the widow and the stranger, and murder the fatherless.

Eze 18:12: Hath oppressed the poor and needy, hath spoiled by violence, hath not restored the pledge, and hath lifted up his eyes to the idols, hath committed abomination.

Heb 13:3: Remember them that are in bonds, as bound with them; them that are illtreated, as being yourselves also in the body.

Mercy on the poor:

Praying for the poor and needy is not sufficient, we should take care of their needs and help them financially.

Pro 14:21: He that despiseth his neighbour sinneth: but he that hath mercy on the poor, happy *is* he.

Be polite to all who work for you and are helpless. Go an extra mile to care for them. Many of us, pay them their wages and never bother to even ask them their problems. My maid is an extremely nice person, she talks very less, do her allotted portion of work and sometimes even when she is not keeping well she attends her work without informing me. It is our duty to see that they are well paid and are happy to help us without any burden of financial constraints. Easy to say difficult to follow, but if you belong to Christ you need to learn to serve others and not always be served.

Mat 5:42: Give to him that asketh thee, and from him that would borrow of thee turn not thou away.

Mat 5:39: But I say unto you, That ye resist not evil: but whosoever shall smite thee on thy right cheek, turn to him the other also.

Mat 5:40: And if any man will sue thee at the law, and take away thy coat, let him have *thy* cloak also.

Mat 5:41: And whosoever shall compel thee to go a mile, go with him twain.

40

Murdering/Conspiracy

Murder is such as crime that is an unforgivable sin. It is an unlawful premeditated killing of one human being by another. Some sins are considered grievous such as adultery, murder, idol worship (without repentance).

1Pe 4:15: For let none of you suffer as a murderer, or a thief, or an evil-doer, or as a meddler in other men's matters:

1Pe 4:18: And if the righteous is scarcely saved, where shall the ungodly and sinner appear?

Gen 4:11; And now art thou cursed from the earth, which hath opened her mouth to receive thy brother's blood from thy hand;

(Gen 4:12): When thou tillest the ground, it shall not henceforth yield unto thee her strength; a fugitive and a vagabond shalt thou be in the earth.

Lev 24:17: And he that killeth any man shall surely be put to death.

Types of murder:

Murder with subtlety:

Manipulation of incidences leading to murder, thought of murdering someone or putting another person in a dangerous area, in order to get rid of him are all intentions of murder. Here is the story of David who lacked peace among his sons. God's punishment inflicted on him was severe. He paid the price for his sin all the rest of his life. God blessed him and because he committed adultery his generations failed. (2Sa 11:15 to 17).

2Sa 12:10: Now therefore the sword shall never depart from thine house; because thou hast despised me, and hast taken the wife of Uriah the Hittite to be thy wife.

2Sa 12:11: Thus saith the LORD, Behold, I will raise up evil against thee out of thine own house, and I will take thy wives before thine eyes, and give *them* unto thy neighbour, and he shall lie with thy wives in the sight of this sun.

2Sa 12:12: For thou didst *it* secretly: but I will do this thing before all Israel, and before the sun.

Gen 9:6: Whoso sheddeth man's blood, by man shall his blood be shed: for in the image of God made he man.

Conspiracy:

They are people who think wrong thoughts and possess wrong ideas and over a period of time execute them. In other words, it is a secret plan by a group to do something unlawful or harmful. Every wrong thought should be put to instant death and the mind should be trained to think only good thoughts. Conspiracy means nursing ideas of destroying someone, putting an end to one's carrier and giving them unnecessary financial losses.

All of these are sins against others.

Gen 37:20: Come now therefore, and let us slay him, and cast him into some pit, and we will say, some evil beast hath devoured him: and we shall see what will become of his dreams.

Other forms of Murder:

Abortion is a form of Murder: The logic behind abortion is irrational. The first point is that every child's birth is Gods handy work through you. If God didn't want you to have a baby, he could have made you barren. Second is the commonest reason for abortions, i.e., unwanted children out of wed lock that means that now you have committed two great sins; adultery and murder. The next reason is when the doctor says that baby's growth is not normal or baby has a defect which push us for an abortion. Fine you have no faith in God and you are a self planner and had committed murder. Next reasons are "I did not want a baby now but it was just an accident" or "I had consumed lots of medicines and hence I am scared if I will have a defective child." Your statements itself indicate your faith in God and how strongly you depend on yourself and on the opinion of doctors and do things contrary to the law of the Lord.

Whatever may be your excuse you have no right to destroy a life that God has made. If you didn't want a baby you should have taken the precautions. No scientific or medical explanations can erase this form of murder as practical living.

Sacrificing kids to idols: In earlier times kids were sacrificed to idols to appease Gods. No true God will ever want a human sacrifice. Even today in remote uneducated areas, children are sacrificed to Gods.

Murdering of Female kids: I have heard that in remote villages female kids, as soon as they are born, are killed by feeding them with rubber milk. It is not common these days as people are getting more and more educated.

Euthanasia: Once a person is old enough and suffering from chronic ailments it's better to let the patient die peacefully at his home with his family. Instead, this person is taken and put on ventilator for a long period of time and finally he doesn't recover and then you decide on (Mercy killing). If you had let God decide the death time he could have died peacefully long time back. Well to put a hopeless case on ventilator is the first crime that many do. Mercy Killing could not have existed if medical science just left God to decide the final end of men, made by God.

41

Coveting

Unusual desire/earning for your neighbours property, goods etc. Money is the root cause of all evil. Every man should be aware that money is an essential commodity for existence and not for the soul. People hold on to money and accumulate it without even shelling a single pie for their brothers or others wellbeing. The basic requirement from mankind by God is how well you can spend your life in this world with kindness, and love for God and man.

You are not assessed for how much you possessed in terms of finance in this world. Every Christian should follow the Bible closely to understand few things. If you have money to live a decent living and be happy, then all your needs will be taken care of by your father in heaven. Amassing wealth to buy a massive house where you alone are going to live in your old age with no loved ones around you or buying a Mercedes Benz which is going to crash out soon are all worldly lust. Instead, if you have enough to live and your poor sister asks you food or shelter for her very existence then you need to help. If you spend lavishly on things that are going to perish with no thought for the poor people that crosses your life daily then your soul is going to be in hell and your generations are going to be poor. Be content with what you have. After your needs are met the rest or a major portion of your income can be spent for the needy so that your coming generations are blessed. Your aim here is to please God and not live as you please. Submit all to God and ask God to grant you wisdom and Godly knowledge so that all shall be well with your soul and you have earned riches in heaven when Jesus returns.

What are the things that can come under coveting?

- Lending money on usury to your own kin.
- Taking gifts which can bias your judgment.
- Stealing another's money or property.
- Taking by force what belongs to another.
- Not giving God tithes.
- Love for money and pleasure.
- Cheating others to gain more money.
- Oppressing the wages of the poor.
- Any wrong way for material gain is coveting.

Few of Biblical examples for coveting:

Mic 2:2: And they covet fields, and take *them* by violence; and houses, and take *them* away: so they oppress a man and his house, even a man and his heritage.

Mic 2:3: Therefore thus saith the LORD; Behold, against this family do I devise an evil, from which ye shall not remove your necks; neither shall ye go haughtily: for this time *is* evil.

Coveting can be money, position, job or anything that rightly belongs to another. Bible clearly speaks of not accepting even gifts because a gift can make you partial and unrighteous. The reason for man wanting to have another man's property is greed. When you are not contented with what you have, when you are not fearful to God and when your understanding of this life here is false then you do all the wrong things resulting in change of priorities in life.

Usury:

Pro 28:8: He that by usury and unjust gain increaseth his substance, he shall gather it for him that will pity the poor.

Eze 18:8: He *that* hath not given forth upon usury, neither hath taken any increase, *that* hath withdrawn his hand from iniquity, hath executed true judgment between man and man,

***Exact no more*:**

Luk 3:13: And he said unto them, Exact no more than that which is appointed you.

Stealing:

Lev 19:11: Ye shall not steal, neither deal falsely, neither lie one to another.

Lev 19:13: Thou shalt not defraud thy neighbour, neither rob *him:* the wages of him that is hired shall not abide with thee all night until the morning.

Eph 4:28: Let him that stole steal no more: but rather let him labor, working with his hands the thing that is good, that he may have whereof to give to him that hath need.

Pro 29:24: Whoso is partner with a thief hateth his own soul: he heareth cursing, and bewrayeth *it* not.

Tithes:(Robbing God)

Pro 3:9: Honour the LORD with thy substance, and with the firstfruits of all thine increase:

Pro 3:10: So shall thy barns be filled with plenty, and thy presses shall burst out with new wine.

Cheating--Wicked balance:

Pro 11:1: A false balance is abomination to the LORD: but a just weight is his delight.

Pro 20:10: Divers weights, and divers measures, both of them are alike abomination to the Lord.

42

Environmental Pollution

An unsightly property next to your house devalues your own house. If we don't maintain our property well then the entire neighbour hood can have problems. This happens when we are anti-social in outlook, or sloppy, or out of station in another country or old age and in lack of good help. On my way to the clinic there is a cattle farm which is not well maintained and while passing that way the stink of cow dung reminds each passerby not to be a public nuisance by not keeping your area clean. This is also the case with pets. If you have a dog and it is not well trained then its excreta will be seen all around and sometimes right in front of your neighbours house. The second problem is tall grass, left untrimmed for many months you can see snakes sliding down from the other property into yours. It can be a danger to the little children playing around the yard. How many children have died of snake bites? The next commonest problem is disposing waste into the neighbours back yard and also accumulating waste in your yard resulting in bad odour. Encroaching on your neighbors property includes examples as the coconut tree fully loaded with coconuts from your yard slanting into your neighbours yard there by increasing the risk of coconuts falling on someone's head. How many times I have seen patients reporting with bruises from free falling coconut/jack fruits in casualty duty postings? Bible clearly tells us that we need to give due considerations to our neighbours and should not harm them in any way. As Christians let us learn to be Godly and understanding in all these matters. God tells us that if someone falls off from your roof, which you have insufficiently barricaded then the fault is yours so imagine, how much more will all the other matters weigh in the eyes of Lord.

Deu 22:8: When thou buildest a new house, then thou shalt make a battlement for thy roof, that thou bring not blood upon thine house, if any man fall from thence.

Lev 24:19: And if a man cause a blemish in his neighbour; as he hath done, so shall it be done to him;

Deu 27:17: Cursed *be* he that removeth his neighbour's landmark. And all the people shall say, Amen.

Mat 22:39: And the second *is* like unto it, Thou shalt love thy neighbour as thyself.

43

Obsessive Compulsive Disorders

This is an anxiety disorder which produces uneasiness, apprehension, fear or to possess certain obsessions and compulsions like washing dishes repeatedly, washing money (notes/coins), over cleaning the house, self etc. They repeatedly check if everything is fine. They are ritualistic, expect perfection and indulge in sex, can have violent behaviour to harm others. These people fear the unknown as death or get the feeling that someone close to them is going to die; they are always anxious and tensed. These people are generally managed by behavioral therapy, medications and sometimes with electroconvulsive treatments. But in Christ we will be given the endurance to go through the tough times and will be carried in the arms of Jesus.

Anxiousness for all matters including your future is also coupled with fear. The only cure is to relax your mind, help others financially, spend time with people who you love and make Jesus your friend. The moment you get anxious or excessively worried about something, close your room and start talking to Jesus. You will feel better.

Mathew 6:34: "Therefore do not be anxious about tomorrow, for tomorrow will be anxious for itself. Sufficient for the day is its own trouble".

2Timothy 1:7: For God gave us a spirit not of fear but of power and love and self-control.

44

Intentionally Harming Other's Property

Intentionally taking someone's property, trespassing, sticking posters or graffiti on another person's compound wall are all intentional harm to neighbours. The examples are putting an advertisement banner, obstructing the house view, damaging the post box, breaking into the house, altering the fence position or boundary wall, growing strong rooted trees very close to the neighbours compound wall to demolish the boundary, etc.

Exodus 22:1 to 31: If a thief is found breaking in and is struck so that he dies, there shall be no bloodguilt for him, but if the sun has risen on him, there shall be bloodguilt for him. He shall surely pay. If he has nothing, then he shall be sold for his theft. If the stolen beast is found alive in his possession, whether it is an ox or a donkey or a sheep, he shall pay double. "If a man causes a field or vineyard to be grazed over, or lets his beast loose and it feeds in another man's field, he shall make restitution from the best in his own field and in his own vineyard.

45

Invention of Evil Things

All invention causing harm to nature, replacing human intelligence are devious in the eyes of Lord. If necessity is the mother of invention, the invention is fine but if acquisitive is the mother of invention then it is harmful.

There are many harmful inventions likes CFCs, Alcohol, Gunpowder, Tobacco, chemical weapons, nuclear reactors and its waste materials, toxic fumes from factories, flame drills which can probably cause earthquakes or volcanoes, computer assisted memory and functions. These inventions harm human race beyond one's imagination. Some scientist were extremely sincere and their invention was for a particular use but devious minded people misused it to kill millions, one such example is Fritz Haber's cheap nitrogen fertilizer that was used to execute almost a million people during the Holocaust.

Another example is Arthur Galston's Agent Orange which killed many people in Vietnam War and still is the cause of many birth defects in Vietnam. I know of an aunty who still refuses to purchase any tea or herbal products made in Vietnam because she claims that the side effects are still lasting. Joseph Wilbrand's TNT which was used as a yellow dye by now was adopted as an explosive. Thomas Midgley's CFC Freon was supposed to be safe and later they realize that it has destroyed the earth by depleting Ozone layer. Dr. Gerhard Schrader's Sarin gas is also in news. Sir Marcus Laurence Elwin Oliphant's heavy hydrogen nuclei later on became hydrogen bomb. This list goes on and if the entire list of inventions are compiled then each of these man made inventions could have at least three side effects documented or yet to be known. As a doctor I have observed the drugs available in the market. Each marketed drug is initially claimed to have the promise of cure with the least of side effects and are being given to patients, after few years these patients report back with adverse effects and then the drug is banned. Man by his inventions has harmed humanity more than helping it.

Ecc7:29: This only have I found: God made mankind upright, but men have gone in search of many schemes."

Rom 1:30: Backbiters, haters of God, despiteful, proud, boasters, inventors of evil things, disobedient to parents,

Daniel 12:4: But thou, O Daniel, shut up the words, and seal the book, even to the time of the end: many shall run to and fro, and knowledge shall be increased.

46

Not Subjective to Another

When you feel that you are not subject to anyone/any regulations you do what you feel like. This is what animals also do. They are not subject to anyone. To be subject to elders and people of authority is not weakness or something you need to be ashamed of. Our Lord Jesus was subject to his parents until the right time for his ministry came. Subjection is obedience and indicates Godliness, it helps in disciplining and prepares us to be a useful vessel to God. A child not subject to his parents will always disregard outsiders and be a trouble in his work place for his superiors. The lessons to be subject to one another, starts at home and continues as a good nature throughout one's life. A man who is proud can never be subject to another. Only a humble and meek person can be subject to one another and such a person is a valuable asset to God and becomes an usable vessel in the hands of God.

1Pe 5:5: Likewise, ye younger, be subject unto the elder. Yea, all of you gird yourselves with humility, to serve one another: for God resisteth the proud, but giveth grace to the humble.

1Pe 5:6: Humble yourselves therefore under the mighty hand of God, that he may exalt you in due time;

Section 3
SINS AGAINST SELF

Introduction

This section on sins against self includes only God and you. Here, our discussion centers on sins that we commit which don't harm anyone except ourselves. Every child of God needs to be aware of the types of sins that could lie dormant in each of us. These hibernating sins surface as we pass through difficulties in our lives, like unknown ailments, miseries, lack of peace, anger, frustrations and bad testimony. These sins can be revealed to us if we pray to God to show us the hidden sins. Once you are aware of these sins, a genuine confession to God can make you a free, happy and peaceful person with the Spirit of the Lord resting within you. The excavation of these sins from self and total freedom from these sins can be achieved only when you accept Jesus Christ as your Lord and saviour. The release from the bondage of self-made sins helps and equips a spiritual man, to be more useful for the Lord's work. To harbor known and unknown sins that often include human mistakes, familial curses and self-proclaimed curses can harm our personal lives and prevent the wonderful blessings that were otherwise ours to enjoy. When does man seek the maker? Either in trouble or in a quest to know God more and more? When you know and understand the heavenly plan you look into yourself and analyze your short comings. Just knowing your shortcomings, sins and weaknesses will not be sufficient to really love God. It requires an effort to get rid of them permanently then only one can love and please God. Our aim is to walk with the Lord as Enoch did. This is near to impossible by your own effort but with Christ in you, it can be made a reality. Sins hinder your prayer from reaching God, sin can leave us unclean, can pervert your ideas about God, can hold back your blessings and the infilling of the Holy Spirit. Are you one of the five virgins prepared for the bridegroom's arrival? We all need to be Christians carrying that extra oil ready to be burned for that unknown hour. Let us embark on this journey to study self and sins. Sins against self can be related to thoughts, actions and words. Any sin that is entertained in mind for a long period of time manifest in the form of wrong actions and rude words. All the sins against self are self-destructive weapons and the sinner is like a suicide bomber. These sins are to be first recognized, confessed to God and we need to ask God for the grace not to repeat the same sin. This will help us to slowly get rid of them without any effort.

Few manifestations of self-made sins are: A sample to recognize these sins

Inferiority complex

- Unable to communicate with people the right way.
- Gets you to be self oriented.
- Friends don't like you or rather tease you.
- While praying other thoughts come to your mind.
- Obstacle filled life.
- Diseases.
- Unhappiness.
- Lack of peace.
- Familial traits with many of the individuals born to that family suffering from same disease through generations or untimely death.

Many of the members of the same family are childless, not married; suffer mental problems, unsuccessful in whatever they do.

Large financial losses, drunkenness, drug addiction, prostitution, gambling, unusual desires, suspicion, not contented with what they have, depending on witchcraft and black magic etc.

47

Wicked Imaginations

Evil thoughts are thoughts that want you to come up in life above others, in all matters such as a promotion in which you devise evil against the immediate contemporary colleague who is equally eligible for this post. You start praying that he fails in some aspect or have an accident or dies or get him defamed. Devising evil ways to get rid of your superiors or friends, manipulating others in your mind to harm them, and cursing them in your mind are few examples. The difference between sin against others and self is that in the latter the other person treats you like a friend and has no clue about your true feelings for him. Generally people devise evil to climb the ladder of success, get more money, get promotions or as a motive to bring down another's honour. The in-depth wish of desiring to have more and more can kill you slowly in action and words. You are dissatisfied with whatever you have in life and put undue pressure on yourself to gain more and more without enjoying the God given life. This unchecked desire of yours to get yourself more gains makes you a work alcoholic. You don't even have time for your own family and friends. Any man who desires in his heart to be rich and spend hours working to be rich without spending time with family and friends is going to have tribulation and anguish, says the Bible.

Types of sinful thoughts that can go through a person's mind are:

- Excessive love for money and the dire desire to have more and more.

- To increase the unwanted comforts and luxuries around you
- To think vainly of a worldly life.
- Lustful sex filled thoughts (committing adultery by mind).
- Perverted thoughts which are unnatural.
- Wanting in thoughts to be supernatural in wealth, courage, affluence, influence and position.
- Pride filled thoughts.
- Wanting to learn more and more for vain glory.
- Evil thoughts to bring down a prosperous friend or foe.
- Evil thoughts to manipulate and control others.
- Wicked thoughts for conspiracy, murder and cheat.
- Wicked imaginations of ruling and dominating the world.
- Day dreaming of useless things.
- Encouraging sinful thoughts that can manifest as sin.
- Pride and vanity that makes you to think you are God-like.

Thoughts that are of worldly love:

A man living his life for money or fame lives for himself and not for others and God. He hurts everyone around him and loves money above all things. It's wise to know that money is just an essential commodity for day to day living and not the very life. You cannot carry wealth along with you when you die. The ideal way could be to help all who ask of you and God shall gratify all your needs. Money is the mammon of this world and should be treated as a slave by spiritual people.

Mat 19:21: Jesus said unto him, "if thou wilt be perfect, go *and* sell that thou hast, and give to the poor, and thou shalt have treasure in heaven: and come *and* follow me".

Mat 19:24: And again I say unto you, it is easier for a camel to go through the eye of a needle, than for a rich man to enter into the kingdom of God.

Heb 13:5: Be ye free from the love of money; content with such things as ye have: for himself hath said, I will in no wise fail thee, neither will I in any wise forsake thee.

1Jn 2:15: Love not the world, neither the things that are in the world. If any man loves the world, the love of the Father is not in him.

1Jn 2:16: For all that is in the world, the lust of the flesh and the lust of the eyes and the vain glory of life, is not of the Father, but is of the world.

1Jn 2:17: And the world passeth away, and the lust thereof: but he that doeth the will of God abideth for ever.

Contentment:

1Ti 6:6: But godliness with contentment is great gain:

1Ti 6:7: for we brought nothing into the world, for neither can we carry anything out;

1Ti 6:8: but having food and covering we shall be therewith content.

1Ti 6:9: But they that are minded to be rich fall into a temptation and a snare and many foolish and hurtful lusts, such as drown men in destruction and perdition.

1Ti 6:10: For the love of money is a root of all kinds of evil: which some reaching after have been led astray from the faith, and have pierced themselves through with many sorrows.

48

Lustful Thoughts

Lustful thoughts include sex in dreams, filthy dreams, mental adultery, etc. Many people who are frank to me share that many times they have killed their wives/husbands in their dreams and has got married to someone else. Lusting after money, beauty and flesh are the sources of adultery, exchanging wives, multiple sex partners, prostitution, gambling, lottery, usury, vain beautification of self, cosmetic surgery, extravagant wardrobes, jewelry, fashion, style, perfumes, sex appeals and so on. Any excessive desire for any of the above is an indication of lustful thoughts. A man who has lustful thoughts is most likely to indulge in these activities.

If you spend too much time in front of the mirror and spent more than half of you're savings in beauty parlour, costumes, perfumes and accessories, you better beware!

Co 10:6: Now these things were our examples, to the intent we should not lust after evil things, as they also lusted.

Jas 1:15: Then the lust, when it hath conceived, beareth sin: and the sin, when it is fullgrown, bringeth forth death.

49

Self-oriented

How many times a day you think about the wellbeing of others? How many times do you lend a helping hand to your brother in need? How many times do you pray and intercede for other people matters? You really need to introspect into yourself. If from morning to night your thoughts revolve around your office work, your children's affairs and your wife's job, your future financial security and bank deposits, you need to change. You need Christ in your life to feel the burden of another brother and his needs. Selfless in everything you do is difficult to follow until Christ and the heaven takes priority in your life. To always keep others and their matters as first priority is only possible in a person who has Christ living within him/her.

Rom 8:27: And he that searcheth the hearts knoweth what *is* the mind of the Spirit, because he maketh intercession for the saints according to *the will of* God.

50

Lack of Prayers

Many years back I happen to read a thought somewhere which read, prayer is the key to open a day and a key to lock a day. I respect Muslims and Jews, for meticulously following strict timings to come into the presence of the mighty God and doing it routinely irrespective of the fact they are tired, in tight situations, when everything goes wrong; they manage to reach on time to attend appointment with God. Our problem is grace, grace will see us through, we need not be disciplined with set timings, but our holy spirit should be in constant prayer. We are wrong in saying that our Lord Jesus spend hours in the presence of God, communed with God constantly and away from the crowds. If Lord Jesus needed these disciplined hours of togetherness with God then imagine how much more do we require?

Mar 1:35: And in the morning, rising up a great while before day, he went out, and departed into a solitary place, and there prayed.

Act 16:25: And at midnight Paul and Silas prayed, and sang praises unto God: and the prisoners heard them.

Col 4:2: Continue stedfastly in prayer, watching therein with thanksgiving;

51

Lack of Peace

1Pe 3:11: And let him turn away from evil, and do good; Let him seek peace, and pursue it.

From the above verse, one truth stands out that we need to make effort to have peace. Let me share few experiences with you. If you don't possess or train yourself to have a good character your whole life will be filled with trouble. Our previous chapter on sin against others clearly project the truth 'treat others as you wish to be treated, if you follow this golden rule you will have peace with others. Now rest of the matters leading to lack of peace includes matters concerned with your thought process. If you can understand the underlying cause for the lack of peace you can tackle all problems with prayer. Taking undue risk on finances is an error, most of us do. Police cases, car accidents, diseases, disobedient children, bossing superiors, nagging wife, drunken husband, drug addicted children, psychological problems, lack of job, difficulty to run a family, mental trauma, congenital deformities, childless, not married, cannot find a suitable partner, bad company, forced into adultery, abuses, physical torture, mental torture, overwork, over anxiety, childhood abuses, guilt, sleeping disorders, taking medications for sleep, fear of closed spaces , water etc. Now I am sure there is no one in this world who doesn't have a problem that always comes to our mind. Some people are blessed with everything in this life but lack the blessing of being loved. Whatever may be your problem I can assure you from my personal experience and counseling sessions for others that we always get an immediate answer from praying earnestly.

Once our burden is placed on Christ, we feel free provided we constantly pray and keep fellowship with the Lord. I have a verse that is placed in my guest room which reads "when the devil reminds you of your past remind him of his future" I always wonder whosoever has quoted it must be a very positive person. Do not let your past affect your future allow not that old thoughts to eat you up. Cut it out from your mind and think of all the nice people you met of all the good things that you have and of all the other blessings in your life. Here are few tips to keep your mind out of trouble. Let me re quote an "An idle mind is a devil's workshop". First point is you need to have a good occupation that you enjoy and like to do. And here are few tips to start and end a day making it worthwhile. Start your morning very early with prayer of gratefulness and ask God to lead you for that day, carry out all the responsibilities laid out on you for that day as if you are doing it for God, try to help at least one person a day who you don't know, pray for people who don't like you, spend at least an hour with your kids and family. If you have old parents call them and talk to them, at the end of that long day have a family prayer with thanksgiving. If you follow the above routine you'll find that you have peace, you are happy in the Lord and your very presence will give people around you a positive energy.

Many times family prayers are too long, you can instead sing a hymn, read from proverbs or psalms and let each of the family member share that days joys and concerns, this will get the entire family including the kids involved in knowing the joys and sorrows of the family. This will help the children get interested in family prayers and also let them know how God is leading your life or else it will be just that they are physically present but spiritually absent.

Heb 12:14: Follow after peace with all men, and the sanctification without which no man shall see the Lord:

Rom 14:19: Let us therefore follow after the things which make for peace, and things wherewith one may edify another.

52

Vain Glory

Is to be boastful, unwarranted pride in one's accomplishments or qualities, it also means ostentatious display. Proud people are people who let their mind think great of their ancestral wealth, family name, education, wealth, influence, political clout and position. They have an aversion to the others of low background. Their eyes are blinded by worldly facts. These thoughts impregnating their minds make them to act and speak in an arrogant way that hurts others. Kids who do well in class also have the same feeling for others who don't do well in exams. The thought "*I am much better than you in all aspects*" is a sin hated much by God because all positions and wealth and the decision to be born into that family and gifts given to each man are determined by God and you have no right to insult God's choice.

One of the greatest sins against self is pride. Pride makes you strut, speaks vanity and God gets displeased with you.

Pride can blind all our senses and sometimes out of folly we even equate ourselves to the almighty by allowing the devil in our thoughts. Many of the people with mental illnesses are people who are proud, boasting, exaggerating or succumbing to dark forces as talking to them & inviting them. Pride begins initially in the thought process. It inflates us to think that, what we have today is something that others don't possess. These thoughts finally come forth as exaggeration, criticism, unkindness, boasting, vain glorying, expecting people to give us respect, and making us mean and selfish.

1Sa 2:3: Talk no more so exceeding proudly; let not arrogancy come out of your mouth: for the LORD *is* a God of knowledge, and by him actions are weighed.

1Pe 5:5: Likewise, ye younger, be subject unto the elder. Yea, all of you gird yourselves with humility, to serve one another: for God resisteth the proud, but giveth grace to the humble.

Pro 16:5: Every one *that is* proud in heart *is* an abomination to the LORD: *though* hand *join* in hand, he shall not be unpunished.

Pro 16:18: Pride *goeth* before destruction, and an haughty spirit before a fall.

Pro 16:19: Better *it is to be* of an humble spirit with the lowly, than to divide the spoil with the proud.

Pro 11:2: *When* pride cometh, then cometh shame: but with the lowly *is* wisdom.

53

Daydreaming

This is a mere waste of time. It's like dreaming things beyond reality. Examples include wanting to be superhuman, to be extremely rich, to do great adventures and to have relationship with others by dreams. These thoughts can trouble you. They distance you from God and hamper your prayer life. They make you to live in your own world with no communication to the outer world. Daydreaming is living in secret sin. Most of the mental illnesses can proceed from this. Result is that you become absentminded, loss of alertness to situation, cold to sympathy, becoming unrealistic, lazy, wasting precious God-given time and have sleeplessness, depression, and aversion to normal things or sleep overtime. You can spend hours on dreaming useless things that are not good for your life or others. But it is recommended that if you have dreams that can benefit any human it is good. Instead of daydreaming, it is favoured by God to act in the direction to fulfill these dreams or else they stay only in your dreams and die with you. All good dreams of use to others are to be executed by acting on ways to fulfill them.

Jud 1:8: Yet in like manner these also in their dreamings defile the flesh, and set at nought dominion, and rail at dignities.

54

Unthoughtful

Unthoughtful means, not exhibiting or characterizing by careful thought. Not thinking of the goodness of our God and no thoughts for the feelings and needs of your immediate family and friends. You don't think of doing the right things at the right time. Sometimes in your thought you know that there is a need to call this person to convey a greeting or for consoling him but your mind is too occupied with other matters that you ignore this thought process this kind of behaviour is termed as being 'unthoughtful'. Thinking of good things that can make others happy and partaking in social needs of others help us to maintain good relationship with others and is well pleasing to God. Let us learn to train our minds and to be thoughtful to the needs of people around us. Blaming God in your mind for the hard situations faced in life is also thoughtlessness. These thought processes land you in depression and you are lost. In this situation, the ability to think in the right manner is diminished. Some people think that every prayer and request made to God should be immediately answered or else they think God is powerless. People get angry with God, murmur against tough situations that are actually their faults. They equate God to a God who is giver of health, wealth and affluence regardless of how they live. It's like you keep a maid in your house who decides what she wants to do for you regardless of what your needs are and what you want her to do for you.

Num 14:27: How long *shall I bear with* this evil congregation, which murmur against me? I have heard the murmurings of the children of Israel, which they murmur against me.

55

Vindictive Thoughts

Few of the believers who pray daily have confessed the feeling of attempting suicide when they are not able to handle family matters. Many normal people at least who feel normal suddenly get an urge to push someone down the stairs or harm them. Some others always have vindictive thoughts against people who try to correct them. But most often all these struggles happen within one's mind and only 10% manifest these thoughts as action and those people are categorized as psychotics. Well, Why do these unwanted harmful thoughts occur? Others complain of frequent dreams of snakes, tsunamis, toilet waste floating and the list goes on. Why do these thoughts come to some people and stick to their mind, also when they possess the sanity to know it's wrong and refrains from executing them. I can only suggest to keep these thoughts that trouble you in fasting and prayer earnestly, help shall reach you in some form. In short, all evil thoughts which is of no good to anyone or yourself, i.e., vain imaginations, proud thoughts, condemning others by mind, murmuring in mind, equaling yourself with God, adultery by mind, dreaming which is of no use, insulting in mind, belittling others, devising evil or having mean thoughts against others, enjoying the calamity that has happened to your enemy or friend in heart but maintaining a sober picture externally or self-condemning and cursing self or others should be evaluated and arrested. Your thoughts are naked to God, who knows every thought which of course, has its own consequences. To get rid of your thoughts which are useless to you and others you need to first know that it is a sin and confess it with true repentance seeking forgiveness and asking God's grace to keep these thoughts permanently out of your mind.

Php 4:8: Finally, brethren, whatsoever things are true, whatsoever things are honorable, whatsoever things are just, whatsoever things are pure, whatsoever things are lovely, whatsoever things are of good report; if there be any virtue, and if there be any praise, think on these things.

To add, one should think only on such things.

Tempting Thoughts:

A desire to do something, esp. something wrong or unwise. You very well know that it is wrong to do or think about it, yet you find pleasure in this tempting thought. You allow it to nest within your mind. Of course, you have the ability to resist it yet you decide that this last time I will think and then tomorrow I will change. It can results in greater sins like adultery, stealing to smoking, drinking, drugs, and lying. Sometimes you vow not to eat any junk food, read a dirty book or see a blue movie yet you yield to that sin because you think everyone does it then why I shouldn't. A constant desire leads to temptation and to sin. Temptation can be overcome only when you let Jesus live within your heart and mind.

The Bible says:

Jas 1:12: Blessed is the man that endureth temptation; for when he hath been approved, he shall receive the crown of life, which *the Lord* promised to them that love him.

Jas 1:13: Let no man say when he is tempted, I am tempted of God; for God cannot be tempted with evil, and he himself tempteth no man:

Jas 1:14: but each man is tempted, when he is drawn away by his own lust, and enticed.

and finally

1Co 10:13: There hath no temptation taken you but such as man can bear: but God is faithful, who will not suffer you to be tempted above that ye are able; but will with the temptation make also the way of escape, that ye may be able to endure it.

56

Self-cursing

Self cursing are curses against self that are uttered casually to strong words proclaiming self-destruction. For example, "*I am sure to get diabetes that runs in our family*" is a casual utterance of disease, which can overpower you. Instead you can pray to God to protect you from the same. Strong words of your own puts you in peril as "*Why the hell was I born into this dirty world, I wish I was run over by a motor vehicle and got killed.*"; *how many nice people die daily, so why not a stupid idiot like me*" etc.. One thing is for sure, God has a purpose for you, ask God what is your role in this world and in which place you are to stay and then stick to your role in allotted place. When God has ordained you to a duty he guides you with ease and there is joy and peace in your heart. Now God is in total control of your life and is able to carry you in his arms through all your troubles as you have handed your life's remote control to God. But if you hold on to the remote control and keep changing channels you invariably miss the important programs in your life and you are lost.

Words are powerful and every word that's uttered which demeans you or your intelligence has negative effects on you. Hence, I have understood that pronouncing such bad statements against your child, such as "*I know for sure that you will end up badly in this world*", or "*you are mentally retarded*", all have bad effects on your kid's life. In anger we use very harsh words on kids, whereas it's better to go into the presence of God and ask forgiveness.

Every tongue should utter good words, and brought to obedience in Christ. Hence let us request God to give us the presence of mind to use our tongue wisely.

Many of us don't intent to speak badly to our children but one must remember that words such as, '*if you go on like this you will have to be a sweeper*' or '*never will improve*' or '*you are the most useless thing I have ever encountered*' are all subtle form of curses that flow from us. We need to realize these mistakes and ask forgiveness of our children and God. Not only that, we also curse people who do not get along well with us, and this is wrong. Bible tells us to love our enemies. And remember, every curse will return back to our own head.

3:6: And the tongue is a fire: the world of iniquity among our members is the tongue, which defileth the whole body, and setteth on fire the wheel of nature, and is set on fire by hell.

3:10: out of the same mouth cometh forth blessing and cursing. My brethren, these things ought not so to be.

57

Feeling of Unworthiness

I am not good for anything. I am a butter finger, whatever I do it turns out to be bad. All my business has flopped, I am not liked by anyone, I don't have the support from any one, and people consider me useless. Why do you feel like this? Was someone discouraging you or not appreciating the good things you do and to top it you don't have the mental strength to have confidence in yourself? Who are these people always criticizing you? Know What God thinks of them. These are the people who think they know everything and can do a job with perfection. They ridicule and belittle, bringing down the self-esteem of others. This makes the weaker brother feel he is good for nothing. God knows them and shall judge them accordingly. But man needs not be bothered about such persons because they are as withering grass and fades away soon. Their brains and knowledge work only if God gives them the grace of tranquility. They don't realize the fact that the very health and intelligence are a blessing from God. Every man needs to ask God to grant him the wisdom and feeling of worthiness. Any spirit contrary to it is from the evil one. The knowledge of God is the beginning of wisdom. Many situations in Bible, as the conversation between Moses and God indicates that Moses considered himself unworthy but God is telling him that he will be given strength and the ability to converse. Good communication, potential to speak and singing are the talents given by God to individuals. It just takes a second for God to bestow upon you any gift that is required for your further service for God. Hence no man ought to be proud or feel self-abased thinking of his plight in any way. Every man just needs to place all matters and his very life for the service and will of the mighty God.

58

Misunderstandings

People who cannot forgive the words or actions or gossip or comments aimed at them suffers from a lot of ailments and hatred to everything within and around them. Always take any comment or gossip in a positive way, either to improve you or to analyze the other person. Forget the incident then and there by keeping the matter in the hands of God. If you have genuinely placed it in the hands of God you forgive that person and though you have understood him you don't hold any hatred towards him. Commit every moment of your life into the hands of the Lord and ask God to grant you the wisdom to handle situations as needed for the glory of God. Never fight to get anything in this world, if it's yours God could bring it to you smoothly. So the golden principle against unwanted comments is to either ignore, forgive or correct you if required, and to never use your tongue for retaliation in self defense.

The other category of people have hard feelings towards others for small matters, for example 'I was sick he didn't even bother to call me and find out how I am', 'I invited him for my daughter's wedding he never came'. These feeling get bottled up in you and give way to an ill feeling towards that person. Always forgive and be happy in the Lord.

Just a word of caution to the believers. Some believers have the uncanny ability to create a misunderstanding between the brothers and sisters in Church and between husbands and wives, they makes a comment that may look like, the husband complained about the wife to her/him and if the wife hears this matter then that night there is no family prayer but verbal fighting. This is also true to some people who think they are good Samaritans by passing on information to another brother or sister regarding how she was talked about by another person in public. If you feel someone is talking bad about another person it's your moral duty to correct him or her pleasantly without transferring this gossip to the person concerned resulting in 'verbal diarrhea'. This term I have borrowed from my husband which he refers to people who spend hours talking about useless things. People who have verbal diarrhea don't lie; they talk what is not necessary. It could be a truth but what sins God has forgiven need not to be discussed or talked. So remember that no one is allowed to remind others of mistakes that he once made for which he has truly repented and God has forgiven. Talking can range from your neighbors' old stories to gossips and also listening to stories which are of no use to you.

People spend days talking on how others can be improved, what are the latest gadgets, on share markets, on fads, on shops, on jewelry and learning celebrity choices and their latest affairs. This is called *killing time.* Apart from this, rest of the time is spent in front of the *idiot box,* reading useless stuff, over sleeping or indulging in perverse activities. The foremost things should be how to improve self in character, how to follow commandments, how to thank God and how to be a useful vessel to many.

1Pe 3:10: For, He that would love life, And see good days, Let him refrain his tongue from evil, And his lips that they speak no guile:

This refers to people who argue on unnecessary topics, issues and words. People dissect the words spoken by another, interrupt it in many ways, sympathizing with self, crying and arguing over it. People argue on politics, family property, and positions and hurt each other with words. People argue on *what I have done for you what you did for me extra.* Bible tells us not to expect anything in return when you do something for another.

Pro 15:4: A wholesome tongue *is* a tree of life: but perverseness therein *is* a breach in the spirit.

Pro 18:7: A fool's mouth *is* his destruction, and his lips *are* the snare of his soul.

Pro 18:8: The words of a talebearer *are* as wounds, and they go down into the innermost parts of the belly.

Most of the people who suffer from blood pressure are unforgiving, murmurers, complainers, with lack of hospitality and criticizers with a temper. Majority of these people suffer from migraine, unknown body aches, body pains and have gastric problems. Bible specifies that if your worst enemy who has been talking very bad about you, gossiping about you, or who has hurt you the most comes under your mercy and all of a sudden you become his boss, Bible tells you to leave the vengeance to the Lord and to treat him honourably. David had many chances to avenge Saul but because David was God-fearing and Saul was once anointed by God, David never hurt Saul.

59

Hypocrisy

It's a habit to compliment people unnecessarily especially when you know that they love compliments. You can call this habit, buttering or smooth talking with an ulterior motive or for some other reason. Whatever may be the reason the Bible clearly tells you to be truthful in what you speak. We support wrong matters, for the fear of isolation from public. We go by opinions harming another person's reputation which is not true. We don't have the courage to speak truth because of the fear of alienation. If we are doing this, to receive other people's appreciation then this makes us a hypocrite. A good Christian should be able to stand for the truth in all situations like Daniel. In my work place, I know a pastors daughter working as an assistant, she pray to the idols and burn incense to the idols to please the management. This is hypocrisy, morning you worship idols and Sundays you go to a believer's church. Never cross the principles in your life to please others you don't get anywhere, because the king's heart is in the lords hands.

Double minded man/Hypocrite

He thinks one thing in mind and does the opposite; assures you of his support but never renders it in need; promises you all help but never to be seen anywhere when you are in trouble. A man who cannot keep small promises such as an appointment, a lending of book, a phone call, a project and so on can never be trusted with big things. A man who cannot keep up time or finish projects as his seniors expected, is a person to whom one cannot depend upon. God will not assign a person any Godly responsibility when he cannot carry out human projects on time. When living in this world if you don't possess the testimony of reliability and dependency then how do you think God will entrust you with a project? Bible says that if you are not faithful in small matters how can you be faithful in big things entrusted to you? I have seen people keep library books beyond authorized dates. You can never be God's trusted children. I have seen people who never reach office on time and blame it on the family. These are just lame excuses and one should remember that God is not going to give him any responsibility either. Genuine reasons are understood and God knows them but not laziness.

Jas 1:8: a double minded man, unstable in all his ways.

Num 14:37: Even those men that did bring up the evil report upon the land, died by the plague before the LORD.

Pro 26:28: A lying tongue hateth *those that are* afflicted by it; and a flattering mouth worketh ruin.

Mat 6:24: "No man can serve two masters: for either he will hate the one, and love the other; or else he will hold to the one, and despise the other. Ye cannot serve God and mammon".

60

Inferiority Complex

Mal 2:9: Therefore have I also made you contemptible and base before all the people, according as ye have not kept my ways, but have been partial in the law.

Sin of not obeying God can lead us to have an inferiority complex. A man who is in constant contact with God always has a feeling of superiority. When you know who you are and how the father in heaven is in charge of all the smallest to greatest matters of your life, you feel that you own the whole world. You need not fear anyone or feel bad of your poor financial or educational background. Remember the disciples with hardly any degree to boast about how wonderfully they preached the Gospel. Just be happy as the person you are. Never even feel that Mr. X or Y is more blessed than me. Once someone asked me, doctor if given a second life who would you like to be, I didn't think much and replied, the very same me. In Christ you have that great feeling of contentment and superiority which only a true believer can comprehend. Inferiority complex can be: lack of good looks, bad in studies, your social status, your job, your attitude etc. If there is anything in your mind that gives you the feeling that I am not good enough than the other person, it is a clear indication that you have failed as a Christian. A Christian is a person who has Christ in him the most superior human form in the whole universe. Because you have not recognized the Christ in you the feeling of inferiority and depression over rules you. Hence, I recommend the readers to get back to Christ, who'll abide within you and give you the very fountain of life. What more superiority do you need?

61

Lack of Communication

You are extremely busy in this world; with your job, your family, your business, and your duties; yet the Bible teaches us to go ahead and take time to console sorrowed hearts, encourage depressed souls, visit bereaved families, advice and counsel troubled souls and be a peace maker in strife. Many times we don't take part in joys and sorrows of our neighbors due to our hectic schedules. We miss the opportunities of love and friendship and stay aloof. Every Christian ought to take that extra effort to reach places where you are needed regardless of your lack of time. You need to make yourself available when visitors come home, when someone close to your family expires, when someone is sick and needs you beside their bedside. Call people you cherish once in a while, maintain good relationships for the glory of God, love your neighbors and be a support to the people in need. God is pleased with you when you take that extra step. It's a sin when you forget to encourage someone or console someone because you are out of the world and do not live according to your heavenly Father's expectations.

13:16: But to do good and to communicate forget not: for with such sacrifices God is well pleased.

62

Giving and Receiving Counsel

Any man who is repeatedly been advised not to do certain things needs to make serious introspection of his behaviour. Many youths take advice with contempt. They either think that the advisor is narrow-minded, conservative or jealous. Every advice given by an older individual or person of higher authority should be considered, thought of and put into practice. We should have a mind to receive council and also discern if the advice is good.

Pro 1:3: To receive the instruction of wisdom, justice, and judgment, and equity;

Pro 1:4: To give subtilty to the simple, to the young man knowledge and discretion.

Pro 1:5: A wise *man* will hear, and will increase learning; and a man of understanding shall attain unto wise counsels:

Pro 1:7: The fear of the LORD *is* the beginning of knowledge: *but* fools despise wisdom and instruction.

Now regarding giving council, often you are asked to give your opinion or advice regarding many matters. All advice and guidance should be given prayerfully and if you are confused regarding your guidance enquire with the Lord or else you will have to answer for your wrong advice.

63

Not Enquiring with the Lord

Enquiring with thy Lord: (ex from Bible)

2Sa 5:23: And when David enquired of the LORD, he said, Thou shalt not go up; *but* fetch a compass behind them, and come upon them over against the mulberry trees.

2Sa 5:25: And David did so, as the LORD had commanded him; and smote the Philistines from Geba until thou come to Gazer.

Keeping promises to God:

Let me try to give few examples of the people who shared with me their experience. Most of the childless couples always vow to God that if you give me a child I will give back the child for Gods services as Hannah did. When finally the child grows up and if the child is not good in studies then he goes to do Lords work and the parents proudly claim that they fulfilled their vow but what if the child is brilliant, just cleared the Indian administrative exams and going to be placed in a high position? Then comes the dilemma, one such mother was talking to me about the decisions she made and how she is regretting it now. After getting his placement the entire family thought that only by Gods grace he has reached here so it is ok to spare him from the vow. The concerned child grown up joined services making everyone happy and totally forgot about God. Basked in delight they deleted the vow from their minds all together. After a few years, he lost his life in a car accident and then his mother said "what belongs to God should be given to him".

I too have this bad habit of making many promises to God and break them often. I will not watch Television, hear music from movies, not eat junk food, will fast this day etc. One day during my quiet time I was reminded by God not to make promises that I cannot keep instead to place my weaknesses into the hands of God in prayer.

Mat 5:33: "Again, ye have heard that it hath been said by them of old time, Thou shalt not forswear thyself, but shalt perform unto the Lord thine oaths":

Here is a wonderful story from the Bible

Jdg 11:30: And Jephthah vowed a vow unto the LORD, and said, If thou shalt without fail deliver the children of Ammon into mine hands,

Jdg 11:31: Then it shall be, that whatsoever cometh forth of the doors of my house to meet me, when I return in peace from the children of Ammon, shall surely be the LORD'S, and I will offer it up for a burnt offering.

Jdg 11:34: And Jephthah came to Mizpeh unto his house, and, behold, his daughter came out to meet him with timbrels and with dances: and she *was his* only child; beside her he had neither son nor daughter.

Jdg 11:35: And it came to pass, when he saw her, that he rent his clothes, and said, Alas, my daughter! thou hast brought me very low, and thou art one of them that trouble me: for I have opened my mouth unto the LORD, and I cannot go back.

Jdg 11:36: And she said unto him, My father, *if* thou hast opened thy mouth unto the LORD, do to me according to that which hath proceeded out of thy mouth; forasmuch as the LORD hath taken vengeance for thee of thine enemies, *even* of the children of Ammon.

64

Lack of Integrity

Promising someone not to reveal a problem of his /her and doing the contrary is a sin. It's good to know other people's problems and share your opinion with them. But if you disclose to another, hurting your friend's feeling, it is a destructive thing to your friend. Never discuss other's problems with your friends or with a third person revealing names and details of the former, and never convey wrong messages about others you heard from hearsays. It will harm their reputation and God is going to judge you for this. Always fear God in whatever you talk and do. Give ear to others and make sure you give good advice and keep the secret in your mind and when it comes to prayer time restore it from your mind and place them before God to find a solution. Once you are done with the problem, never remember it again.

Same way you make lots of promises to people around, like I will help you with the chores, I will buy you that goody, toy, book etc. I will mail you soon, will keep in touch with you always, will daily pray for you, will always remember you, will come home to meet you, will call you for dinner sometime, will help you financially when in need, well you can depend on me, will look into the matter, will recommend for you, will call you often so on and on. But how many of us remember to keep the promises we render? Bible says honour your words that you promised to do .

Promptness/Reliability/Faithfulness/Thankfulness:

Bible speaks of faithfulness time and again and I always feel that faithfulness is the main key to open the Bible scriptures. An unthankful man can never be a believer. If you are a true believer you have to be faithful in all matters. The first thing man needs is faithfulness towards God, if you are thankful and faithful to God you automatically becomes a faithful person in all matters.

Faithful to family- Many neglect their families and don't do the required duty towards their families. And some remain thankless to parents and kin who have struggled in making you, who you are today.

Faithful to your job—half-heartedness to one's job, working only for the salary and not putting your 100% into the job. Bible says that when you are entrusted with a job, you should do it like you are doing it for God.

Faithful to friends—Many times your friends need you badly for a moral support but you are very busy with something that's not an immediate priority. Many of us are lazy to go that extra mile or lose our nap time or TV time or cricket game, to be with our friend in need.

Faithful to your words and promises—Often times, we promise others monetary help, prayer support but forget about the incident as soon as we have said it. God hates people who talk and don't execute promises. It's better not to give false hope, because on that very basis you are going to be judged. Another weakness in our sinful nature is to forget people who were instrumental in making us, who we are today. I have seen people who borrow things and money and never even bother to return it or carelessly lose it without any shame.

The moral of the whole story is 'blessed is a man who has a faithful friend who will stand by you in all your troubles and worries'.

Pro 25:19: Confidence in an unfaithful man in time of trouble *is like* a broken tooth, and a foot out of joint.

1Co 4:2: Here, moreover, it is required in stewards, that a man be found faithful.

A faithful man is contend with his wages, is just and is reliable.

Exo 22:26: If thou at all take thy neighbour's raiment to pledge, thou shalt deliver it unto him by that the sun goeth down:

Exo 22:27: For that *is* his covering only, it *is* his raiment for his skin: wherein shall he sleep? and it shall come to pass, when he crieth unto me, that I will hear; for I *am* gracious.

Luk 16:11: "If therefore ye have not been faithful in the unrighteous mammon, who will commit to your trust the true" *riches?*

Luk 16:12: "And if ye have not been faithful in that which is another man's, who shall give you that which is your own?"

Thankfulness:

Luk 17:15: And one of them, when he saw that he was healed, turned back, and with a loud voice glorified God,

Luk 17:16: And fell down on *his* face at his feet, giving him thanks: and he was a Samaritan.

Luk 17:17: And Jesus answering said, "Were there not ten cleansed? but where *are* the nine?"

Luk 17:18: "There are not found that returned to give glory to God, save this stranger"

Responsibilities/Duties:

It's our moral duty to carry out all responsibilities bestowed upon us with faithfulness and patience. This includes family responsibility, student responsibilities, husband and wife and parental responsibilities. It's our duty to find time slots for each and balance life by sparing time for important matters. It's also our responsibility not to cheat anyone intentionally.

Lev 19:35: Ye shall do no unrighteousness in judgment, in meteyard, in weight, or in measure.

Luk 3:14: And the soldiers likewise demanded of him, saying, And what shall we do? And he said unto them, Do violence to no man, neither accuse *any* falsely; and be content with your.

65

Untruthful/Lying/Boasting

Some people consider lying to be a normal phenomenon. To live they say you can lie if it doesn't harm others. Bible tells that God is watching over your words and always honour's a righteous man. Lying can be to escape a tight situation when you are about to be fired, when your prestige is at stake or for hiding a bitter truth. Sometimes lying can hurt others. God judges you by what you do. If you have lied to save your skin then next time you can get caught for a different reason. If you have lied about others, you are going to get a tougher punishment from God. If you have carried false tales about others you are going to stand in front of the judgment seat. Any words, which are not true regarding yourself or others, are punishable offence.

Pro 12:22: Lying lips *are* abomination to the LORD: but they that deal truly *are* his delight.

Pro 13:5: A righteous *man* hateth lying: but a wicked *man* is loathsome, and cometh to shame.

Boasting:

I have had colleagues who talk on their achievements and trumpet on their knowledge of the subject. They claim to have done tall things by mere hard work and no presence of God. The dialogues they render goes like this, *"A man can reach any heights if he is organized, hardworking, meticulous and persevering of course with will power"*. Its only 10 percent God and the rest of the effort are from us. But, Bible clearly states that it's hundred percent God and if God goes before you then your paths will be cleared of obstacles and you'll be able to complete the project with the least effort.

One of the lessons that God taught me in this life is firstly, to enquire with the Lord before venturing into any project and secondly, to depend only on God to clear all obstacles in the path. If you wish and do things within the will God has for you, you shall succeed in all what you have started. Never boast on things you achieved because whatever you have done is with the grace of God and remember that all things that you have done today shall only glorify God.

Pro 25:14: Whoso boasteth himself of a false gift is like clouds and wind without rain.

Pro 27:1: Boast not thyself of to morrow; for thou knowest not what a day may bring forth.

Pro 27:2: Let another man praise thee, and not thine own mouth; a stranger, and not thine own lips.

66

Not Interceding and Speaking to God for Others

You are a privileged child of God, as you have known the truths. Now it's your moral duty to pray for perishing souls around you. Instead of giving tracts and speaking Gospel through loud speakers you can keep the families of an entire unsaved neighbourhood in prayer and fasting, (a powerful weapon for every Christian in the Lord). Prayer can open all the closed doors for the Gospel. God has specified that the Gospel should not be preached callously instead it should be preached only after tremendous prayer, only then the eyes of men can be opened. These days there is a hate campaign against Gospel preaching and this is because all the humdrum of preaching is without sufficient prayer. No man with his own effort can convert a soul from idol worship. Only the Spirit of the Lord can move the idol worshipper to quit worshipping idols. Hence it's mandatory that every Gospel or tract distribution be done prayerfully and by the guidance of the Holy Spirit and not otherwise. If you are not mocking the mighty God of Abraham and proving yourself to the gentiles as a man who forces conversion.

Many conventions are conducted with jarring loud speakers disturbing the peace of public. Instead of loving your God the disturbed crowd will rather prefer not to follow a *lousy* God. Our God is a peacemaker and is soft spoken. Instead of all the talking and preaching, our mighty God wants His true believers to follow His doctrine to live a life of testimony.

I vividly remember the story narrated by an uncle in our assembly while preaching. The story goes this way-- one poor believer tried to attend a worship meeting. The pastor told him not to enter because his worn out attire might cause disgust amongst his highly honored group of believers. He sadly left the assembly and was standing outside, another man who was a stranger approached him and enquired as to why he is sad, the poor man replied that he was not permitted an entry into this assembly because of his worn out clothes, to which this stranger replied *why be sad; they didn't let me in either*. The poor man enquired to who this stranger was and to the poor man's surprise the stranger replied, brother I am the very Christ.

Spirit of God:

Rom 8:14: For as many as are led by the Spirit of God, they are the sons of God.

Rom 8:16: The Spirit itself beareth witness with our spirit, that we are the children of God:

Rom 8:26: Likewise the Spirit also helpeth our infirmities: for we know not what we should pray for as we ought: but the Spirit itself maketh intercession for us with groanings which cannot be uttered.

Rom 8:28: And we know that all things work together for good to them that love God, to them who are the called according to *his* purpose.

67

Self-planning

Many actions give us away. Only a true child of God with Christ in him can exhibit the right behaviour at all times. A hypocrite who acts to be righteous will be exposed of his true self at one point of time. When we close our eyes to the basic necessities of our dear brothers and sisters', we are going against the second greatest commandment, i.e., love your brother as how you love self. Whatever be the struggle of your brother you as a Christian need to ease his problem out depending on his need either by a word of encouragement, physical presence, financial help, and prayer or by using your official authority. A man who is not concerned about the struggles of another is not a true Christian. True Christians needs to act and think like Christ in all aspects. When you don't lift your finger to help someone in need especially when you are in a position to do so it becomes sin.

Self-Planning:

When people make future plans without praying or consulting God, they are in deep trouble. It will be like building a house all by self without taking expertise from engineers, masons and carpenters. The house you make by self will take years to complete and at the end it will not be perfect and you won't enjoy living in it. On the contrary, the house you build with expert advice and help, gets completed on time, you are not burdened and the construction finishes beautifully. All plans should be put in prayer before you jump to proceed with it and even the very minor decisions should be consulted with God. All plans in your life are the supreme decision of God; any counter plans not in the book of the Lord will backfire with much pain and hurt. God is the best planner for you because God sees and knows you till your death. God knows your talents, capabilities and weaknesses and only burdens you to the extent you can bear. If you plan your life without God you get hurt, cheated and lost.

The greatest example for not waiting for God's time is portrayed in the life of Sarah, for the haste she showed against God's will. Self planning without Gods council, not patient enough to wait for the time, lacking faith in the promises of God are going to cause disruption of blessings in your life. They are many pious people who self planned God's blessings and commit sins; few examples from the Bible are Abraham and Sarah, Rebecca and Jacob, all of them though strong in faith, hastened to fulfill Gods plan by themselves and the result was and is still remains a disaster.

1 Co 2:6: Howbeit we speak wisdom among them that are perfect: yet not the wisdom of this world, nor of the princes of this world, that come to nought:

1Co 2:7: But we speak the wisdom of God in a mystery, *even* the hidden *wisdom,* which God ordained before the world unto our glory:

68

Friendship with Unbelievers

Bible repeatedly warns us not to be friends with evil people, drunkards and hot tempered persons, regardless of religion, race or culture. Evil people are those who commit adultery, murder, are drunkards, looting widows of their possessions, abusing orphans, and people who lend money on usury. Do not be friends with them. Some people claim that you can keep them as friends but you need not be like them but Bible tells us to flee from them. Do you know greater or the best things about you than what God knows? If you make them your friends their habits shall eat into you or if they break any law and are caught then all his friends including you are going to suffer. Your life is going to be like him and you are going to be punished for the sin you never did but as you're his friend and you never listened to the words of God, you will suffer for your friend's mistakes. Most of the child abuses occur when your family friends are not believers and you let your children move freely with them, let your children stay overnight in their house or go for camps and picnics. When you don't select good friends, your children suffer abuse at their hands and for that you are going to be judged by God. Now a days it is not safe for children to be let free or even to let them stay at cousins or sisters place. Hence, exercise caution and be able to discern between good and bad people and ask God to help you to be alert for your safety and for the safety of your family.

Jdg 16:17: That he told her all his heart, and said unto her, There hath not come a razor upon mine head; for I *have been* a Nazarite unto God from my mother's womb: if I be shaven, then my strength will go from me, and I shall become weak, and be like any *other* man.

Jdg 16:18: And when Delilah saw that he had told her all his heart, she sent and called for the lords of the Philistines, saying, Come up this once, for he hath shewed me all his heart. Then the lords of the Philistines came up unto her, and brought money in their hand. And you know the rest of the story. Shame and Death was his end.

Another example is King Hezekiah who showed his atheist, friendly king all the treasures of Israel for which the Lord was displeased and the punishment was that the Lord gave the family of Hezekiah into the hands of Babylonian king. The mistake of Hezekiah from our view point is very small but the Lord punished him for what he did. So how much more should we be punished who daily entertain evil people amongst us.

2Ki 20:13: And Hezekiah hearkened unto them, and shewed them all the house of his precious things, the silver, and the gold, and the spices, and the precious ointment, and *all* the house of his armour, and all that was found in his treasures: there was nothing in his house, nor in all his dominion, that Hezekiah shewed them not.

2Ki 20:16: And Isaiah said unto Hezekiah, Hear the word of the LORD.

2Ki 20:17: Behold, the days come, that all that *is* in thine house, and that which thy fathers have laid up in store unto this day, shall be carried into Babylon: nothing shall be left, saith the LORD.

2Ki 20:18: And of thy sons that shall issue from thee, which thou shalt beget, shall they take away; and they shall be eunuchs in the palace of the king of Babylon.

What an end for a glorious king who merely entertained the wrong people in his life

Those who are prostitutes, murderers, drunkards, idolaters, covetous and extortionist are people who can put you in trouble. Friendship with these people is like cancer and will kill you slowly.

The proverb '*show me your friend and I will tell you who you are*' is an apt proverb. Murderers include people who repeatedly abort their babies too.

1Co 5:9: I wrote unto you in my epistle to have no company with fornicators;

1Co 5:10: not at all *meaning* with the fornicators of this world, or with the covetous and extortioners, or with idolaters; for then must ye needs go out of the world:

1Co 5:11: but as it is, I wrote unto you not to keep company, if any man that is named a brother be a fornicator, or covetous, or an idolater, or a reviler, or a drunkard, or an extortioner; with such a one no, not to eat.

Pro 23:20: Be not among winebibbers; among riotous eaters of flesh:

Pro 23:21: For the drunkard and the glutton shall come to poverty: and drowsiness shall clothe *a man* with rags.

2Ti 3:3: without natural affection, implacable, slanderers, without self-control, fierce, no lovers of good,

2Ti 3:4: traitors, headstrong, puffed up, lovers of pleasure rather than lovers of God;

2Ti 3:5: holding a form of godliness, but having denied the power thereof: from these also turn away.

69

Worldly Pleasures

I remember a classmate who would go to any extend to make money; he started it by taking commissions and later lending money on usury. Few years later made a palacious house, ceased many buildings from customers who were unable to pay back huge sums on usury and later got married to a wealthy girl. When I saw him, he was extremely happy and in seventh heaven. But I could notice from his words that he has changed a lot, he talked more of his present high political contacts, his fame and his dream of becoming an invincible reputed politician. Somehow, I didn't like this new person; I preferred talking to that old vibrant classmate, extremely frank in nature and this very fact I also mentioned to him. I got an indignant reply stating that I am an Ostrich with head in the sand to which I replied, thank God I am not a toothless lion. Many years passed by and one day I met him at the post office but now he was looking old and haggard. Seeing me he smiled, I saw his arms he was suffering from psoriasis. After enquiring on each other's wellbeing he finally asked me where he could find a cure for the dreadful psoriasis. I said Jesus and he mocked at me. Later, I heard from someone that he is completely cured and doing the Lords work but I haven't met him after that. Any money making scheme or greed for more comforts is a sin. These are sin's that affect you and your immediate family. Here are few examples from Bible:

Gen 13:10: And Lot lifted up his eyes, and beheld all the plain of Jordan, that it was well watered everywhere, before the LORD destroyed Sodom and Gomorrah, even as the garden of the LORD, like the land of Egypt, as thou comest unto Zoar.

Gen 13:11: Then Lot chose him all the plain of Jordan; and Lot journeyed east: and they separated themselves the one from the other.

Pro 15:27: He that is greedy of gain troubleth his own house; but he that hateth gifts shall live.

1Co 10:6: Now these things were our examples, to the intent we should not lust after evil things, as they also lusted.

Jas 1:15: Then the lust, when it hath conceived, beareth sin: and the sin, when it is fullgrown, bringeth forth death.

22:26: Be not thou *one* of them that strike hands, *or* of them that are sureties for debts.

3:2: For men shall be lovers of self, lovers of money, boastful, haughty, railers, disobedient to parents, unthankful, unholy.

70

Escapism

Escapism/Blaming Others:

Escapism is the tendency to seek distraction and relief from unpleasant realities, esp. by seeking entertainment or engaging in fantasy. When there is no real healing of your heart and mind you deviate to daydreaming, fantasies, drinking and smoking. When our inner man is hurt and we cannot forget this hurt then we start blaming others including God for the present situation. Later, these problems start eating our soul. If one feels self pity, irritability towards others even if they are not doing anything wrong, intolerance, resentment, anger, oversensitive, hard to forgive, feeling that no one loves us or we are not wanted by anyone, irresponsible behaviour, irrational expectations, perfectionism, hopelessness, obsessive compulsive disorder, hostility, driving one's selves beyond capacity, introvert, and bottled up feelings; then they try to escape from reality. So, escapism is to divert attention from problem, as if the problem is nonexistent, rather than solving the existing problem one find other means like over sleeping, overeating, drinking, pornography, smoking and other addictions.

Here the basic thing is to first make a list of all the irritants and hurts in your life. With this list you keep each matter in prayer and ask God to guide you. God will immediately send a councilor or will speak to you from the Bible verses. There will be a crucial time after the prayer when you are at peace but continue your constant prayer and one day you're realize that you are a free person. Amen

1 Peter 5:7: casting all your care upon him for he careth for you.

Col 3:15: and let the peace of God rule in your hearts, to which also ye are called in one body: and be ye thankful.

71

Destroying Health

I have observed drunkards closely for over ten years. One fall into this dark pit of drinking habit when he/she find it difficult to say NO to friends. It was started for fun but lands up in deep trouble. Most of the drunkards abuse their families, turn violent, beat others, kill people accidently, land in jail and further they become psychotic and most of the chronic drunkards take antidepressants or other psychotic drugs to carry on with their day to day life. They end up losing everything. This is the same story for drug addicts too. Many have succumbed to AIDS and their families have deserted them. Bible says drinking is a foolish decision; it makes one poor, adulterous, perverse, and even forgetting the law. Be not among them says the Bible.

Pro 20:1: Wine is a mocker, strong drink is raging: and whosoever is deceived thereby is not wise.

Pro 21:17: He that loveth pleasure shall be a poor man: he that loveth wine and oil shall not be rich.

Pro 23:30: They that tarry long at the wine; they that go to seek mixed wine.

Pro 23:32: At the last it biteth like a serpent, and stingeth like an adder.

Pro 23:33: Thine eyes shall behold strange women, and thine heart shall utter perverse things.

Pro 31:5: Lest they drink, and forget the law, and pervert the judgment of any of the afflicted.

Hab 2:5: Yea also, because he transgresseth by wine, *he is* a proud man, neither keepeth at home, who enlargeth his desire as hell, and *is* as death, and cannot be satisfied, but gathereth unto him all nations, and heapeth unto him all people:

Eph 5:18: And be not drunken with wine, wherein is riot, but be filled with the Spirit;

72

Over-eating/Gluttony/Obesity

Eating disorders are abnormal habits which includes over eating /under eating which in turn affects individual's physical/mental health.

Now to give the readers the awareness of the attitude of people to the worldly habits it would be appropriate to mention the various ailments coming under this category. So let's read a little on medical terms.

Anorexia Nervosa—fear of gaining weight reason social appearance, media projection of thin models as ideal, biologic or genetic components may be involved. What can happen — bone loss, loss of skin integrity, increases risk of heart attacks and death?

Bulimia Nervosa—characterized by recurrent binge eating followed by self-induced vomiting, excessive use of laxatives/ diuretics, or excessive exercise.

Binge eating—Compulsive over eating

Rumination, (regurgitation, rechewing and reswallowing) Diabulimia, (Manipulating insulin levels to control weight) Orthorexia nervosa, (Pure diet obsession) Pregorexia (Vigourous exercise after pregnancy) and drunkorexia (Restrict food and reserve for alcohol)

Now I need not elaborate on this aspect as any sane individual reading the definitions would know what to call this!

Pro 23:21: For the drunkard and the glutton shall come to poverty: and drowsiness shall clothe *a man* with rags.

Num 11:20: *But* even a whole month, until it come out at your nostrils, and it be loathsome unto you: because that ye have despised the LORD which *is* among you, and have wept before him, saying, Why came we forth out of Egypt?

Num 11:33: And while the flesh *was* yet between their teeth, ere it was chewed, the wrath of the LORD was kindled against the people, and the LORD smote the people with a very great plague.

Eat healthy food including vegetables, pulses and fruits. Have a routine exercise regimen and avoid tensions in life. Involve in hobbies like gardening, painting, etc., and most importantly pray. Many of the staunch believers believe that obese people cannot be pastors or elders. Only if you maintain a healthy body will you have a sound mind goes the saying. Eat what is essential and healthy.

73

Hardness of Heart

You repeatedly hear the Gospel, see men/women who are role models yet you harden your heart to the truth. You are not willing to leave the old habits and prefer to live a worldly life, fully aware of the consequences and after math. This is called arrogance. Arrogance makes you feel that, why I should change my life I am living like 90% of the population and this is more practical. You only have heard of eternal life but not lived it so how do you know it's good. What is the fun in living this beautiful life like a monk so enjoy your life? (This is what the world pronounces). But I pray all to let the heart of Christ be instilled in each of us so that we are not hard hearted to the true words of Gospel. Hardhearted people mercilessly kill their unborn children and profess practicality. Only the love of Christ can change us, to be of understanding and of pure heart. Godly love helps us to love everyone. This is a situation in which you are repeatedly being told the truth of Gospel or are advised on your decisions, yet you are unable to go on the right path because either you fear criticism, isolation by others, or you try to please others and hold on to manmade doctrines. Hence, you are unable to go by the true laws. God calls it hardness of heart. You are told not to do idol worship, not to commit adultery, to keep the Sabbath and many other commandments in the Bible, yet you falter because you are not bothered to make the right decisions or the effort to come out of your sins. God says the easy way out of sin is to ask God for forgiveness and God will definitely give you the grace to do the right thing, welcome Jesus into your heart and take the Lord's help at every stage. But many are unwilling to do even this.

Mar 10:5: And Jesus answered and said unto them, "For the hardness of your heart he wrote you this precept".

Mar 6:52: For they considered not *the miracle* of the loaves: for their heart was hardened.

Mar 7:6: He answered and said unto them, "Well hath Esaias prophesied of you hypocrites, as it is written, This people honoureth me with *their* lips, but their heart is far from me".

Rom 1:26: For this cause God gave them up unto vile affections: for even their women did change the natural use into that which is against nature:

Rom 1:27: And likewise also the men, leaving the natural use of the woman, burned in their lust one toward another; men with men working that which is unseemly, and receiving in themselves that recompense of their error which was meet.

74

Choosing Evil Neighbourhood

Few things we need to understand about people who don't believe in the mighty God or fear him is that, the protection of the Lord is not upon them. We can also get harmed along with them because over a period of time we imbibe the culture and practices from them and our next generation merges with them. Let us look at some examples from the Bible.

Of those people who sought to live among the evil people was Lot. God mentions about the unrighteous and evil ways of the people of Sodom. The place you stay and make your abode matters. Make sure you stay in a neighbourhood approved by God, where people are God fearing. Lot moved to stay with the most evil people, built a house there contrary to the commandment of the Lord, married his children to the people there, against the laws of the Lord, his wife was money loving and finally a sinful generation was born to Lot and to this day God calls them the sinful nation.

Gen 19:14: And Lot went out, and spake unto his sons in law, which married his daughters, and said, Up, get you out of this place; for the LORD will destroy this city. But he seemed as one that mocked unto his sons in law.

75

Destroying Nature

This is a constant topic of discussion amongst my friends and finally they tell me that I am not practical. The arguments start from depleting natural resources and contaminating them. My friends argue that this is science progressing and I adamantly add to that the progress is at the expense of natural resources which God has stored for many generations to come. What you use from stone to all the main ingredients for any type of construction, comes from nature. While depleting them the entire morphology of land gradually change, mountains are no more, plains get deeper, trees are cut down, excessive tiling around house prevents water from sinking into ground thereby reducing the water table, climatic alterations occur. Beautiful stretches of green land turns to vast deserts. Natural disasters occur due to excessive mining of sea bed and digging bore wells. Smoke from factories pollutes the air we breathe and in totality we live in a poisoned environment. The list is endless, scientists have developed new grains which are pest resistant, new vegetables which has longer shelf life, everything is altered now what do you call all this. In conclusion, most of the present ailments and natural calamities are manmade. Even the water pollution is increasing at an alarming rate because of the excessive use of chemical detergents and cosmetic products, adding to the already existing problems. Let me end with few Bible verses indicating the care God gives to nature and even the birds.

Deu 22:6: If a bird's nest chance to be before thee in the way in any tree, or on the ground, *whether they be* young ones, or eggs, and the dam sitting upon the young, or upon the eggs, thou shalt not take the dam with the young:

Deu 22:7: *But* thou shalt in any wise let the dam go, and take the young to thee; that it may be well with thee, and *that* thou mayest prolong *thy* days.

Deu 22:9: Thou shalt not sow thy vineyard with divers seeds: lest the fruit of thy seed which thou hast sown, and the fruit of thy vineyard, be defiled.

Deu 22:10: Thou shalt not plow with an ox and an ass together.

Lev 19:19 : Ye shall keep my statutes. Thou shalt not let thy cattle gender with a diverse kind: thou shalt not sow thy field with mingled seed: neither shall a garment mingled of linen and woolen come upon thee.

76

Consumption of Unnecessary Medication

Taking medications left and right, drug dependence, abuse of pain killers, Self treatment, and fear of diseases (Hypochondriasis). Minor symptoms can get you upset thinking it to be some chronic illness. Coming to the fear of things for every alphabet there is a listed phobia. And in my calculation if any one died at an early age with kidney failure or liver cirrhosis, just take out his medical history and you will know that he was consuming a handful of medicines in morn noon and before going to sleep. And I am positively sure that of all the deaths 75% is by drug misuse. My mother was a hypochondriac, if she feels that she would catch cold she immediately pops in an antihistamine and if someone with a common cold comes home, she does the same in anticipation of catching cold. Medicines should be taken wisely and after praying. I call this generation a Pill popping generation from birth till death you thrive on pills. To get pregnant, not to conceive, to have sex, to go to bath room, to ease tension, to get sleep, to increase memory, to be less active, to reduce sleep, to eat, to loss appetite, to reduce weight, to be resistant to infections, to get confidence, to have stamina, and what not. I think soon the food we eat also will be in tablet form. Already many of the attires are in tablet form. Man is increasing in knowledge of science. I turned back the pages of history to analyze the previous generation, the days of my grandparents, without calculator they used to do mental mathematics of big sums easily but now a days my son tells me what's the point in learning all this after all we can do big sums with calculators and every shop has computer billing system. My mother knew all most all the phone numbers by heart but now a days if you accidently lose a mobile phone with no back up I am sure you can hardly remember your residence phone number too. Yes, science is progressing but mens mental ability and yield strength is decreasing. In another ten years there will be a generation; not knowing calculations, cooking, agriculture and how to work. A generation of computers with no feeling and natural affection. Excellent to note that science is progressing and Gods creation is going to be extinct from its true form because science will alter men to be disease resistant and disease free soon. For curing any disease the present generation should look to God foremost for healing and then to the available resources. Many of us run to the doctor first and pray that the doctor gets the wisdom. Some people take money and sell their bodies for human trials. If you know the heart of God, you will understand that God is weeping over his creation.

Diseases:

Bible has recorded many known diseases of which majority mentioned are due to sins. For all diseases, Bible asks the Israelites to consult the chief priest and make atonement. Most of the diseases are manmade or as a result of sin.

Sores, scabs, leprosy, paralysis, mental disorders, plagues have all been recorded in the Bible. For every disease the causes are two: one, your sins, or God. God allowed Satan to form boils on Job's body, as part of testing Job's faith but gave Job the grace to pray and wait on the Lord.

In today's world manual jobs have drastically reduced. Instead, man works sitting on his chair without straining the body yet feeds himself like a manual labourer, this allows diseases associated with sedentary lifestyles such as diabetes, blood pressure and high cholesterol to creep upon him. These are rarely seen in physically active labourers. If man could follow all the commandments including the type of food to eat as taught by the Bible, manmade diseases would be rare.

The next category consumes large number of drugs in form of medicines and new diseases as kidney dysfunction sets in. Abuse to our body in any form, internal sins or external sins as overuse of perfumes and chemicals for bleaching can cause skin cancer and many allergies. A prayerful man subjecting his body to the Lord following the commandments is less likely to suffer from ailments.

If partaking of the Lord's Supper is done with sin, man is likely to have sicknesses and sleep excessively.

Diseases observed related to sin (this is merely based on my observations of people over 16 years need not be due to sin in all the cases)

Asthma----- worldliness, gossip, fashion.

Paralysis-----murmurs, complainers, bitterness and unforgiving,

Mental disorders-pride and daydreamers

Skin disease-------Sexual sins, bitterness, self-sympathizers,

Diabetes, BP, cholesterol-------excessive eating, obesity

Sleepiness----- breaking the Lord's commandment and dreamers, idol worship

Laziness--------lack of prayer

Irritable, excessive anger---------money loving, worldly, self-righteous

Leprosy and other genetic disorders-----------sins from generations as adultery, murder, idol worship

Bareness-----stubborn, haughty, sins

Blind deaf and dumb—lascivious or generational sins

Any problem should be first taken to the best Physician, God who will tell us the solution and by confession and prayer most of the diseases can be cured. If tested by God, God gives the abundant grace to survive it.

Mar 2:9: "Whether is it easier to say to the sick of the palsy, *Thy* sins be forgiven thee; or to say, Arise, and take up thy bed, and walk?"

77

Hypnotizing

Hypnotizing is to put a person to hypnosis, charm or beguile. It is experiencing a form of trance, an altered level of consciousness. It is to mentally confuse the conscious mind so that it simply becomes easier to just relax and let go into hypnosis. Though they say hypnosis is not harmful some people can get addicted to it. Every Christian should know if this procedure is of any worth. Mental relaxation can be easily achieved by praying instead of hypnosis.

Rom 12:2: Do not be conformed to this world, but be transformed by the renewal of your mind, that by testing you may discern what is the will of God, what is good and acceptable and perfect.

Black Magic:

Different types of black magic from mind reading, Telekinisis (to move physical objects with mind power), Vodoo, pinning the doll, manthras, occult, talking to dead and intentional harming of a targeted person. What are the intentional harms a black magician can do?

The list is surprising and here are the few

All sorts of head ache, epilepsy, stomach pain, joint pain, unusual body pain etc. Disrupting the family life, finance, children and giving them unusual liking to abnormal things can all be done through black magic. From the ancient days black magic is prevalent and still continues.

Based on vengeance someone can do the above things to you or intentionally you get involved in dark magic. Any science or magic that harms others or causes a confusion of your sane mind should be avoided. All dark magic is done by satan/jin or idol worshippers, all these people can do water witching, levitation (the lifting of one's body in the air with no support), dowsing to use a divining rod (a forked stick alleged to dip downward when held over an underground supply of water), table tipping, psychometry (devination through objects), healing by witch doctors (a person who practices primitive medicine as among the tribes in Africa).

Isaiah 8:19: And when they say to you, "Inquire of the mediums and the necromancers who chirp and mutter," should not a people inquire of their God? Should they inquire of the dead on behalf of the living?

Lev19:31: "Do not turn to mediums or necromancers; do not seek them out, and so make yourselves unclean by them: I am the Lord your God.

Lev 20:6: "If a person turns to mediums and necromancers, whoring after them, I will set my face against that person and will cut him off from among his people.

78

Fashion of this World

In those days, only teenagers used to follow the latest fads. In the present generation at every age people go after fashion. Let's dwell into this topic in detail. People like to look good

- For acceptance by others
- To attract others
- To lure others.

This accounts for the number of male and female beauty salons. Everyone likes to outdo the other in glamour. The latest trendsetters include all sorts of weird hairdos, dyes and bleaching, to the piercing of various body parts.

Bible specifically tells us not to tattoo or pierce our bodies. Your body is a spirit filled tabernacle.

Now next is the way you dress. Attires that expose your body attracting attention should not be worn for a church meeting. Any dress that draws attention of the audience or public should be avoided. How you dress is your testimony with the Lord. By luring others by your dressing and action you upset a new believer and send in the wrong message. But the mighty God is going to weigh your every action.

Many times when worldly men threaten us, a fear engulfs us. Fear can be due to peer pressure in a young age tempting to live the worldly way contrary to how your Christian parents taught you. For example, you don't want to or are not comfortable in wearing something but you force yourself to wear the same because it's the latest fashion which is accepted by your colleagues. Kids should be taught not to yield to bad habits as smoking, drinking, past time affairs, calling dead spirit and witch craft under peer pressure. Parents should give a clear picture of the consequences all these can bring to their lives. Every sin done during teenage or school with bad company of friends has its repercussions.

Isa 3:16: Moreover the LORD saith, Because the daughters of Zion are haughty, and walk with stretched forth necks and wanton eyes, walking and mincing as they go, and making a tinkling with their feet:

Isa 3:17: Therefore the Lord will smite with a scab the crown of the head of the daughters of Zion, and the LORD will discover their secret parts.

Lev 19:27: Ye shall not round the corners of your heads, neither shalt thou mar the corners of thy beard.

Lev 19:28: Ye shall not make any cuttings in your flesh for the dead, nor print any marks upon you: I *am* the LORD.

1Co 7:31: and those that use the world, as not using it to the full: for the fashion of this world passeth away.

Deu 22:5: The woman shall not wear that which pertaineth unto a man, neither shall a man put on a woman's garment: for all that do so *are* abomination unto the LORD thy God.

79

Lazy/Procrastination

A lazy man is one who wastes his time for useless things in taking knowledge of this world via TV or computer. He thinks great of his abilities but brings no good to his soul. There are many types of lazy people: one who does not earn but spends his time gambling and drinking and whatever little income he gets he squanders it without attending to even the basic needs of his family. Another type spends a lot on extravagant things but takes care of the needs of his family but doesn't save for his future or coming generation. God calls him a man of no understanding. The last type earns, saves but leaves his own soul to starvation due to his laziness to pray and ultimately all that he earned and saved is lost to people who never worked for it. This shows that everything earned should be by God's grace or else the succeeding generations doesn't enjoy the fruits of your labour.

Pro 6:9: How long wilt thou sleep, O sluggard? when wilt thou arise out of thy sleep?

Pro 6:10: *Yet* a little sleep, a little slumber, a little folding of the hands to sleep:

Pro 6:11: So shall thy poverty come as one that travelleth, and thy want as an armed man.

Pro 10:4: He becometh poor that dealeth *with* a slack hand: but the hand of the diligent maketh rich.

Pro 10:5: He that gathereth in summer *is* a wise son: *but* he that sleepeth in harvest *is* a son that causeth shame.

Pro 10:26: As vinegar to the teeth, and as smoke to the eyes, so *is* the sluggard to them that send him.

Pro 12:24: The hand of the diligent shall bear rule: but the slothful shall be under tribute.

Pro 13:4: The soul of the sluggard desireth, and *hath* nothing: but the soul of the diligent shall be made fat.

Pro 19:15: Slothfulness casteth into a deep sleep; and an idle soul shall suffer hunger.

Pro 20:13: Love not sleep, lest thou come to poverty; open thine eyes, *and* thou shalt be satisfied with bread.

Instruction manual made by man for man states that Homo sapiens (term for humans) are meant to enjoy the comforts of AC room (is to do white collar jobs). But Gods manual for the sons of God indicates agriculture, herding, gardening etc.

Whatever job you are involved in you need to work hard on it and earn your living out of your job. You are not here to make easy money. Bible gives us examples of the life of an ant. Pastors and elders should not depend only on the tithes for livelihood but should work for their own income in some constructive or creative way. (As stated by Apostle Paul)

2Th 3:8: neither did we eat bread for nought at any man's hand, but in labor and travail, working night and day, that we might not burden any of you:

2Th 3:9: not because we have not the right, but to make ourselves an ensample unto you, that ye should imitate us.

Pro 13:11: Wealth *gotten* by vanity shall be diminished: but he that gathereth by labour shall increase.

Not only is laziness related to work but putting away work for tomorrow is also a sin. Procrastination is the mother of laziness. We need to complete our responsibilities and duties the same day, without fail unless and until, we are in an unavoidable situation.

80

Lack of Discipline

I have seen many people spending hours doing jobs which are good for nothing. These people do things without any planning. Our elder generations used to plan every day. A day's planning should start with God first. Then the entire day's work will go smoothly. First priority in this life should be given to God's plans and purposes for you.

The next priorities are to the duties you are assigned to do. Every duty should be done as if you are doing it for God. Equal priority should be given to family matters. Works out of schedule can pop up and if it is within the will of God you need to find time to do them too. At the end of the day you should thank God for all the good things you were able to do. Every day should begin from the presence of God and end in the presence of God and every moment of your life you should thank God for all His loving kindness.

Such a person will neither go wrong in the decisions he or she makes nor deviate from the commandments of the Lord and in all the days of his life he shall be a living testimony for man and God.

Jer 10:2: Thus saith the LORD, Learn not the way of the heathen, and be not dismayed at the signs of heaven; for the heathen are dismayed at them.

81

Self-righteous

These people think that whatever they have done so far is perfect and what others do is silly. The most wisest thing an unbeliever does will be converted to foolishness and most silly thing that a believer does will be for good.

The basic thing any man ought to know is that he is not God and nothing he does is perfect. A self-righteous man will be put to shame because he depends on his abilities and thinks his decisions are wise. Whereas a God fearing man takes counsel from God and falls at the mighty feet of God and request for a better life, and allows God to make decisions for him, I can guarantee you that any decision made by a righteous God fearing man in the long run will not fail though it will look silly to the so called wise.

Luk 18:13: "And the publican, standing afar off, would not lift up so much as *his* eyes unto heaven, but smote upon his breast, saying, God be merciful to me a sinner."

Luk 18:14: "I tell you, this man went down to his house justified *rather* than the other: for every one that exalteth himself shall be abased; and he that humbleth himself shall be exalted."

Partaking in lords table with unconfessed sins:

Only a self righteous man will come into the presence of God with hard feelings and a stubborn heart. It is said that if you have argued or fought with someone, ask them for forgiveness and then come into the presence of God. Never ever come to God with an unforgiving sinful heart. A sinful soul cannot sit in the presence of the Lord and pray; hence guard your soul from sin lest you move away from God. Never answer back people who are shouting at you or calling you names. If you talk back then you have failed. Better to keep quiet and save your soul. Many times we take our mighty God lightly with no respect for him. Few things as believers we need to do is to prepare ourselves before partaking in the Lords table. How do I do it? Our mind should be free from bad thoughts and hard feelings towards others. In short it is said that unless your vertical relationship with God and horizontal relationship with man is well maintained you should think twice before partaking the lords table.

1Co 11:29: For he that eateth and drinketh, eateth and drinketh judgment unto himself, if he discern not the.

1Co 11:30: For this cause many among you are weak and sickly, and not a few sleep.

Mat 5:23: "Therefore if thou bring thy gift to the altar, and there rememberest that thy brother hath ought against thee;"

Mat 5:24: "Leave there thy gift before the altar, and go thy way; first be reconciled to thy brother, and then come and offer thy gift."

82

Lack of Faith

It's each individual's mindset that measures the faith parameter. Many of us pray verbally without any confidence that this person can be healed by God's grace. Most of us believe in fate. They say that if everything is written on head and already preplanned by God then why do we need to pray. If Moses had thought that way, the entire nation of Israelites could not exist. Through many intercessory prayers many of God plans can be changed if he feels you are asking for a righteous cause. When Nineveh repented, God turned from his anger. You as a Gods child have the privilege to discuss matters with God and intercede and pray for lots of matters but with faith. Every Christian should be a fruitful vessel to God and to the society he lives.

Jas 1:6: But let him ask in faith, nothing doubting: for he that doubteth is like the surge of the sea driven by the wind and tossed.

Jas 1:7: For let not that man think that he shall receive anything of the Lord;

1Co 2:5: That your faith should not stand in the wisdom of men, but in the power of God.

Good vessel:

2Ti 2:21: If a man therefore purge himself from these, he shall be a vessel unto honor, sanctified, meet for the master's use, prepared unto every good work.

1Th 5:6: so then let us not sleep, as do the rest, but let us watch and be sober.

1Th 5:8: But let us, since we are of the day, be sober, putting on the breastplate of faith and love; and for a helmet, the hope of salvation.

I have seen people who just live for themselves with no concern for any one.

They are fruitless. A good Christian is known for his good works. When God made you his child then you are supposed to look around you to help others, console others, pray for others and bear good fruits if not you will be hewned down like the fig tree.

Mat 21:19: And when he saw a fig tree in the way, he came to it, and found nothing thereon, but leaves only, and said unto it, "Let no fruit grow on thee henceforward for ever". And presently the fig tree withered away.

Mat 21:21: Jesus answered and said unto them, "Verily I say unto you, If ye have faith, and doubt not, ye shall not only do this *which is done* to the fig tree, but also if ye shall say unto this mountain, Be thou removed, and be thou cast into the sea; it shall be done."

83

Misuse of Inheritance

It is fine to store up treasure for your use and help people in need. It is also Godly wisdom to maintain your inherited properties wisely for the use of coming generations. When you spent extravagantly on useless things and sell out all your land for a pittance and become debtors it becomes a sin. Some people venture into big profit business in hope of earning double guided by wrong people and finally loss all their properties as debt. It is a sin to misuse the treasures and talents handed over to you from generations by Gods grace. A just man thinks about his generations and uses his wealth wisely. He fills his life with good deeds and leads a Godly life. I have seen parents spending lavishly on cars and building mighty complexes for vanity. Talking of the misuse of inheritance I am reminded of the prodigal son. Many vises can deplete you of your ancestral wealth but Christian living can give you the clarity of mind of what to do and what not to do. Hence I humbly remind the readers not to sell your ancestral properties for material gains or extravagant spending. Do not keep your property on mortgage for foolish reasons or on wrong advice. It is very difficult to regain what you lost in this world. But to people who have lost everything, do not worry there is still hope in Christ who can redeem you out of all your debts and restore you fivefold but only if you follow him faithfully and not expecting anything.

Mat 6:19: “Lay not up for yourselves treasures upon earth, where moth and rust doth corrupt, and where thieves break through and steal:”

Mat 6:20: “But lay up for your selves treasures in heaven, where neither moth nor rust doth corrupt, and where thieves do not break through nor steal:”

Mat 6:21: “For where your treasure is, there will your heart be also.”

84

Money Lending

Mortgaging and loan:

They take loan beyond their capacity and slog lifelong for useless things. A wise man uses his land wisely with Godly wisdom and enquires of the Lord of all his passions if it be of God's will. He spends his life constructively by making just what is required for his basic needs and saves the rest for his coming generations. Landed properties are an asset that the older generation cherished but the newer generation disposes of inherited lands without any hesitation and buys commercial complexes in prime localities which is not wise. You can make commercial projects without selling or mortgaging your landed properties to banks. Lands always remain asset to mankind and cultivable land in any form should be maintained as a God given treasure. Amassing more and more lands and wealth at the expense of the poor man or undue attachment to your properties is a sin.

Pro 13:22: A good *man* leaveth an inheritance to his children's children: and the wealth of the sinner *is* laid up for the just.

*Exo:22:*25: "If you lend money to any of my people with you who is poor, you shall not be like a moneylender to him, and you shall not exact interest from him.

85

Abasement

I have heard people saying statements like, *I have a donkey's brain how can I ever think of completing this task; I am so ugly looking; see my crooked teeth, my dark complexion*. Basic thing man needs to understand is that your creator is not a fool to make you the way you look and you have no business complaining about anything. If you are still feeling bad about anything, it's advisable to keep it in prayer. It is better to request God to help you overcome that particular problem and to give you the wisdom and confidence to handle the problem in your life. Every situation in life should be taken positively with the assistance of God. A person who submits every matter in prayer will be victorious and will have that inner peace that passes all understanding. I have seen people who are handicapped but very confident about themselves and are self-sufficient.

God has made each one of us perfect for our families and place. Every celebrity who indulge into plastic surgery to look different, suffers the pain and require constant medications and extra care further medical help to remain the same. What a pain? A normal man has peace of mind, a happy family but no money to bash, just sufficient money to live. Be contented with whatever you have and be happy in this life the way you are and then you notice that you will be the most envied person because you possess the peace and happiness which others don't have.

Php 4:7: And the peace of God, which passeth all understanding, shall guard your hearts and your thoughts in Christ Jesus.

86

Manipulative

We live amongst a crooked and perverse generation and it is difficult to gauge the motives of other people. But the subtle devious mind of many gets exposed most of the time. It is better to keep away from people who are manipulative and who can cheat you. God recommends us to have the heart of a dove with a sharp mind to discern between bad and good. Many bossy and arrogant people can take advantage of your decency. They are pushy enough to drive their ideas into your minds. God has given us the wisdom to understand them and put your foot down firmly on matters without getting pushed around. You need to develop a firm nature within, to speak out and say no I am not for it. Be straight forward in all matters and let your dealings be transparent and your answers be yes or no. Never cheat anyone in weights or have an ulterior motive in friendship. In our language they say "you will be used like a curry leaf and be then thrown out'. This is a leaf used in curries for flavor; it is not consumed but just kept aside and thrown out. If you make friends with people for their money, resources, and contacts or for getting married to his/her sister or brother. Your mind is devious and God hates a devious person. Your friendship is with a motive which is a sin in the eyes of the Lord. Remember Jacob he had a devious mind and landed up with a devious man and payed as many years of service for his pushy attitude.

Deu 27:19: Cursed *be* he that perverteth the judgment of the stranger, fatherless, and widow. And all the people shall say, Amen.

87

Childlessness

Children are a gift from God. People who are childless need to ask God first rather than seeking all the infertility treatment humans can offer. Whatever treatment you do, God has to bestow his kindness for a barren womb. Biblical incidences of bareness cured by God are Sarah and Hannah. God worked on them to open their wombs. In today's world man uses all his wisdom to get a baby, injects countless number of medicines and it becomes a money making industry. The natural process of child birth is slowly getting shut out, why? Can be due to sin?. Issac entreated for Rebecca to God and God heard his prayers. If God heard Issac he is a living God and still able to hear us if we call upon him. An example of barrenness related to sin

2Sa 6:20: Then David returned to bless his household. And Michal the daughter of Saul came out to meet David, and said, How glorious was the king of Israel to day, who uncovered himself to day in the eyes of the handmaids of his servants, as one of the vain fellows shamelessly uncovereth himself!

2Sa 6:23: Therefore Michal the daughter of Saul had no child unto the day of her death.

Or might be that God has a specific plan and wants someone to willingly offer his/her child for Gods ministry like Samuel

1Sa 1:5: But unto Hannah he gave a worthy portion; for he loved Hannah: but the LORD had shut up her womb.

Now what should the present generation do? Many of my friends are childless and I have witnessed their sorrow and the depression they undergo in their life. But most of them initially took contraceptives so that they can enjoy their initial married life without children and after some time when they wanted a child it never happened. Hence the golden rule here is if God gives you a child take or else be prepared to bear the consequences of your decisions in this life.

88

Accumulating Knowledge

Many years back I happened to visit a mental hospital, the reason was that one of my colleagues lost her mind due to academic pressures. The learning system in India is such that you cannot pass the professional course with ease. The passing criteria are stringent in good universities. Many candidates repeatedly fail either the theory or practical's, still the parents pressurize them to somehow complete the professional course. I always tell them this is the greatest mistake they are making; every child born into this world cannot be a doctor hence the choice of a professional course should be solely left to the interest of the child. Well unfortunately this is not so and many are unable to even complete their tenth grades and many drop out from courses and go insane and many get addicted to alcohol and drugs, what a waste of life. Aiming to be a professional, giving undue stress to invent or accumulate knowledge finally makes us go crazy. Hence it is recommended that only students with caliber who are able to take studies without mental stress should take up such courses. Well back to the hospital visit I managed to collect data of few of the inmates about the source of their insanity, the reasons varied from psychological trauma from child abuse to excessive knowledge, religious fanatics, and drug and alcoholic addicts. This visit was a great eye opener for me and I learned that accumulating too much knowledge that the mind cannot withstand is dangerous. I also met an interesting person who was a doctor, well versed in scriptures as he saw me he started preaching and finally threatened me that if I don't accept Jesus as my saviour I am going to face death. Religious fanaticism is extremely dangerous. The concept that until you convert the entire world into the doctrine to the extent you feel right or else destroying it completely is against the biblical law. Our duty is to convey the Gospel to the nations with prayer and not threatening any one to convert to Christianity. Teasingly my cousins used to ask me hey you are born again, ah do you have an extra bone somewhere, I used to wittingly say yea a support bone called Christ to straighten my spine as most of us living in this world act spineless. (lacking resolution, weak and purposeless)

Gal 2:6: But from those who were reputed to be somewhat (whatsoever they were, it maketh no matter to me: God accepteth not man's person) - they, I say, who were of repute imparted nothing to me:

Ecc 1:18: *For in much wisdom is much grief: and he that increaseth knowledge increaseth sorrow.*

Can academic degrees make me a better person to mankind or increase my spiritual knowledge or give encouragement and good feeling of Christianity to others. Is my present job and position a glory to God? Is my testimony favoring Godliness in me? Is my position beneficial to many in any form? All these questions need to be answered before you waste time on excessive learning. Prophet Daniel was knowledgeable to the extent that he found favour with the king. Knowledge comes from the Lord. Stuffing with all the theories of this world, which does not benefit anyone, is not productive knowledge. Wisdom and true knowledge always comes from God. Man out of human wisdom today tries to alter and modify genes leading to grave consequences. Human wisdom is just doing something for fame and pleasing men. If the world is going to continue experiments in this form, future generations are not going to see any of the vegetables or plants we eat or see now. More risk of new diseases and altered genes, which can destroy the normal human resistance to diseases, also can be formed. Ultimately man will have plenty of money, houses and all comforts but no food to eat and water to drink.

2Ti 3:7: ever learning, and never able to come to the knowledge of the truth.

89

Prejudiced/Intolerant

Having or showing a dislike or distrust that is derived from prejudice which involves discrimination, partisanship, narrow mindness, etc.

It's human nature to judge and make assessments about people. Discerning between good and bad people is God given wisdom but judging or condemning another man on the basis of his religious belief, looks, quietness, or mannerisms is not right. When initially I was offered to be taught the Bible, I had two friends accompanying me to hear the Bible discourses too. Compared to the other two I was more modern in outlook, dressed in the latest fashion and was decked with ornaments. To every change of clothes I had matching studs, shoes and accessories. Near the Christ Church there were two elderly people living. In my early days I used to visit the local congregation with two of my friends to hear the Bible being explained.

After looking at me, one of the elder sisters in that congregation tried to counsel me on the need to dress more modestly many times and one day I heard another believer an older woman rebuke her with these words: "Why do you want to recite the scriptures into a buffalo's ear?"(Commonly said in the South for people who are unlikely to change their old habits). I, the so-called buffalo, remained silent on hearing this but by the grace of God remain in faith to this day. Ironically, the two other friends did not and due to family pressures went back on their commitment to God.

Often, we tend to judge people by their external appearances. The soul is known only to God, hence we should not pick and choose to whom we tell the Gospel. Very often God uses the "buffaloes" of this world that we condemn as not mature or fit enough, for his glory more than the saints that we perceive to be of more benefit to the kingdom of God. It is our basic nature to criticize everything around us from the food we eat to the government policies. We judge our elders in our assembly and point fingers at them for their petty faults, also when you are worse than them. This is called judging. It is a sin to find fault or condemn others, contrary a good Christian stands in the gap and gives sound advice and prays for the fault to be rectified in turn gently showing him/her the right path. It's clearly indicated in the Bible, not to judge another person's actions or words and proclaim punishment. Let God grant us the wisdom to speak and act as Godly children with love.

Rom 14:4: Who art thou that judgest another man's servant? to his own master he standeth or falleth. Yea, he shall be holden up: for God is able to make him stand.

90

Do Not Fear Men

To please men, don't forsake principles and morals and close your eyes to injustice.

Devout Christians close their eyes and promote idol worship in form of hefty donations to temples and pronounce that all religions are one and the same. Can men pleasing make the world a more beautiful place? Not so, God is one and in the form of a Spirit and truth and if you are a true Christian you need to live by the word of our Lord. Christians who support gay rights, genetic alterations, abortions, prostitution, and euthanasia can please men around them but the punishments that come from God is scarier than pleasing men around. We need to fear God above all. Look at the long-term judgment God will give when we'll stand in his presence. All that's in this world is going to perish but the soul stays and is going to be judged based on what values we lived for. Everything in this world has been made to work for the benefit of men by the supreme sacrifice of our Lord Jesus Christ.

Never live this life to please another as he is not going to save your soul. Never please others for monetary benefits, or for fearing of losing your life or by threats. God is going to leave you to the lust of this world. Imagine your mighty creator discarding you or turning away from you on judgement day. It's like a mother who abandons her baby.

Heb 13:6: So that with good courage we say, The Lord is my helper; I will not fear: What shall man do unto me?

During adult life we fear losing jobs, fear of isolation by colleagues so we have a tendency to be luke warm in matters of righteousness. Also the fear of evil forces comes due to the fact that we have no idea of how God works and protects. Fear of the unknown, fear of getting beaten or succumbing to harmful men should not be entertained.

Many times, I have had to refuse donations to temples. This is because I don't believe in any form of idol worship. Many of my colleagues call it foolish, as it is not wise to displease certain party's people because they can harm us. But remember one thing; God is above all. Which is more harmful, temporary displeasures from people or permanent displeasure from God? Always fear God that is able to kill soul and body above mammon. A good Christian fears for nothing except losing his soul.

One fine day a Pastor walks into the clinic. After the dental procedure I asked him how are you guided by God to speak on the pulpit, you stick to the prepared topic or the holy spirit guides you to speak on something? The reply "Oh Doc I generally prepare my topic beforehand it is very difficult to be reminded of something there and to preach. The reasons are: one your flow of the preaching will not be perfect; secondly the holy spirit sometimes remind you on smoking, adultery, divorce, regarding touchy subjects people don't like to hear about which I cannot preach because when I look up I see brother X who donates the maximum to our congregation, He is divorced three times and also 25% of teenagers smoke and it's very difficult doc and you know I ain't a saint" Pastor completed his dental procedures and left back to U.S. God shall judge him.

Mat 8:26: And he saith unto them, "Why are ye fearful, O ye of little faith?" Then he arose, and rebuked the winds and the sea; and there was a great calm.

1Th 2:4: but even as we have been approved of God to be intrusted with the Gospel, so we speak; not as pleasing men, but God who proveth our hearts.

91

Unhygienic

Just because you are child of God you cannot take hygiene and mannerisms for granted.

Every Gods child should maintain good personal hygiene. Well kempt hair, neat dress code, clipped hand nails and toe nails, good oral hygiene and above all Godly mannerisms. In one of my conference journey, I came across a short man with unkempt hair, supposed to be wearing a white kurta now looking near to yellow, broken and carious anterior teeth and dried out feet with long nails and needless to mention the slight garlic smell emanating when he was speaking. He came and sat next to me and smiled and asked me "are you a believer I can see that you are not wearing ornaments". With reservation and hesitatingly I nodded. He introduced himself a chief pastor of a congregation. I merely nodded because I was put off by his mannerisms. He sat next to me sipping tea loudly, the sipping sound exceeded the sound of the running train. By now people around me was keenly watching him and few of the young boys started commenting too. He tried to make friends with people around him and of course conveyed the Gospel too. By now I started praying that God please let the next stop be his but fortunately or unfortunately he travelled the whole trip with me till the final destination. By now an elderly lady sitting to my other side started talking back to him. She was a catholic and felt insulted when he mentioned that the image of Jesus is not of Jesus but someone else as the Jesus in some European countries has blue eyes, some other countries green and in India Black eyes so who is the real Jesus. An argument triggered off luckily the husband of this elderly lady ended the entire argument with one dialogue. He was a respectable looking bespectacled elderly man who was reading a news paper but glancing up from the paper, now and then to observe the reactions to the argument that was going on, after a while the argument intensified to the point that there were many onlookers keenly observing the entire scenario then the elderly man gives a long penetrating look at the pastor, folded back the newspaper, gently placed it back into his suitcase pouch and casually in a normal tone asked the pastor "so is this Jesus you worship as shabby as you or worse than you if so we don't mind worshipping the Jesus with many colored eyes as far as he has one". The conversation came to a sudden stop and immediately the pastor muttered something under his breath and got up and sat in the two seater opposite to us and by now we had reached the final destination and I jumped out. While at the exit of the train doorway the elderly man standing behind me queried 'do you go to the same church as him' and I said a big no and he replied back "good for you a real filthy culture less fellow". Dear brothers and sisters let us be dignified in our speech, dressing and mannerisms so that it doesn't reflect badly on our Lord.

92

Show Off/Looking at the External Appearance

Marriages are conducted to display wealth and status, whereas it should be considered as a covenant with God. These days many functions are just waste of money and time but these functions can be made into a thanksgiving occasion to the Lord.

Never think low of your colleagues based on finance or family position or looks. But treat the poor and rich alike. Never use finance to take revenge on anyone. Display of wealth as a show-off is a sin. Wealth given to you by God is meant to help the poor, give financial support to Gods work etc, and not meant to be a factor of pride. Man looks at the outward appearance but God sees the heart.

1Jn 2:15: Love not the world, neither the things that are in the world. If any man loves the world, the love of the Father is not in him.

1Jn 2:16: For all that is in the world, the lust of the flesh and the lust of the eyes and the vain glory of life, is not of the Father, but is of the world.

1Jn 2:17: And the world passeth away, and the lust thereof: but he that doeth the will of God abideth for ever.

1Sa 16:7: But the LORD said unto Samuel, Look not on his countenance, or on the height of his stature; because I have refused him: for *the LORD seeth* not as man seeth; for man looketh on the outward appearance, but the LORD looketh on the heart.

Not only man gets carried away with external appearances, finance, looks, style, family background, education but also admire such people beyond the love for God. Another problem many of us face is that, we do a lot for the less fortunate but most of our charity work is known to people around us. Bible says even your right hand should not know what the left hand does. Hence all what we do should be in secret and not for publicity stunts that include healing ministries also. The testimony should come from the healed person only.

Mat 6:1: "Take heed that ye do not your alms before men, to be seen of them: otherwise ye have no reward of your Father which is in heaven."

Mat 6:2: "Therefore when thou doest *thine* alms, do not sound a trumpet before thee, as the hypocrites do in the synagogues and in the streets, that they may have glory of men. Verily I say unto you, They have their reward."

Mat 6:3: "But when thou doest alms, let not thy left hand know what thy right hand doeth:"

Mat 6:4: "That thine alms may be in secret: and thy Father which seeth in secret himself shall reward thee openly."

93

Preaching Gospel to All

The Gospel should only be preached based on the guidance of the Holy Spirit and by support of prayer. Any thought of preaching, conventions, or Godly work should be after praying and supported by prayer.

Note that only prayer can give you the infilling of the Holy Spirit; to speak the right words, touch the heart of many and cause them to ponder over what you said and make a permanent impression in their hearts. Without prayer you will be talking in a beautiful language that is good to hear but doesn't form a lasting impression on the people's mind. A speech or word with no God in it is like pouring water over Lotus leaves. It doesn't stay on.

Once you hold the intention of telling the Gospel to someone, first, keep the matter in prayer, ask God for the correct time and words and wisdom to start the conversation. Many a times when I feel like telling the Gospel, I ask God to create a situation or if it be your will, *God today let this concerned person ask me what born again means*. The moral of the story is to keep the matter in prayer before telling Gospel to anyone.

Large processions and loud preaching in residential areas should be banned. Every man should understand that the God of Bible is a peace loving God and never provokes another for fights. Hence, the crude methods of monetary conversions prevalent indicate that you are converting humans without touching their souls. Bible says that men would like to follow your God when you have the peace, love and joy in your life and when you become a living testimony. People accept your God with love and then change their attitudes. Many assemblies make too much noise while worshipping. Let me make this clear, God tells that if a new man walks into your assembly he should know what's happening. Sometimes, I have attended worships that say Halleluiah and amen so loudly that I was not able to hear what the pastor was praying and the worst part is that the Amen is said even before he completes a prayer request. What was the believer agreeing to? Songs end up in tongues and clapping and sometimes also screaming. The Bible has clearly stated the ideal way of how to worship, why go contrary to Gods laws. Every prayer request should be clearly understood by all and at the end the crowd should say amen, as said in the Bible.

1Co 14:23: If, therefore, the whole church be assembled together and all speak with tongues, and there come in men unlearned or unbelieving, will they not say that ye are mad?

1Co 14:24: But if all prophesy, and there come in one unbelieving or unlearned, he is reproved by all, he is judged by all;

1Co 14:25: the secrets of his heart are made manifest; and so he will fall down on his face and worship God, declaring that God is among you indeed.

1Co 14:26: What is it then, brethren? When ye come together, each one hath a psalm, hath a teaching, hath a revelation, hath a tongue, hath an interpretation. Let all things be done unto edifying.

1Co 14:27: If any man speaketh in a tongue, *let it be* by two, or at the most three, and *that* in turn; and let one interpret:

1Co 14:28: but if there be no interpreter, let him keep silence in the church; and let him speak to himself, and to God.

1Co 14:29: And let the prophets speak *by* two or three, and let the others discern.

1Co 14:33: for God is not *a God* of confusion, but of peace. As in all the churches of the saints,

1Co 14:34: let the women keep silence in the churches: for it is not permitted unto them to speak; but let them be in subjection, as also saith the law.

1Co 14:35: And if they would learn anything, let them ask their own husbands at home: for it is shameful for a woman to speak in the church.

1Co 14:39: Wherefore, my brethren, desire earnestly to prophesy, and forbid not to speak with tongues.

1Co 15:23: But each in his own order: Christ the firstfruits; then they that are Christ's, at his coming.

Mat 7:6: "Give not that which is holy unto the dogs, neither cast ye your pearls before swine, lest they trample them under their feet, and turn again and rend you."

1Th 2:5: For neither at any time were we found using words of flattery, as ye know, nor a cloak of covetousness, God is witness;

94

Impatience

Unable to wait or tolerate delay, restlessness, irritability, etc.; it is in us humans to hurry matters, get anxious over pending jobs. Get irritable for trivial things that does not go the way we planned, hates delays, and loves everything to be prompt and on time. We always want to finish of a job before proceeding to another or expect an immediate reply to a question. The present generation is impatient to wait longer in a queue, for a dental appointment and even in an ATM counter. They avoid places where there are longer queue and prefer less crowded places. Often times the commonest complain believers tell is 'I have been praying for this matter for so many years now I am quitting because I am impatient'. Jesus clearly said that only persistent, constant and sometimes by fasting and praying certain things can be achieved. We cannot hurry God to do in our time, we have to patiently wait for Gods time and some of the prayers that we offer need not be God willing. The commonest reasons why prayers are not answered are:

1. A request not God willing.
2. Not submitted to God in the format Jesus taught us. Every prayer should be addressed through Jesus to the heavenly father.
3. Sins in our life that mar the blessings.
4. Not Gods time yet.
5. Some decision of your has obstructed Gods plan and purpose.

6. You are asking for something without taking Gods training (As Moses was trained for forty years to lead Israelites).
7. During the training sessions you fail the trials and temptations required for your prayer request.
8. Lack of faith that God can do it for you.
9. Your unbelief.
10. Testing God.
11. Your request of this matter can lead you to lose eternal life.

On all the above matters there is a delay in our prayer being heard? Now how to know what to pray, one's closeness with God and one's guidance by Holy Spirit enables him/her to discern between what to ask in prayer and what not to ask for. Our problems are such that we pray and wait and sometimes many years pass by without an answer, we are disheartened and lose interest in prayer and sometimes being impatient back slide from faith too. It is God's grace that we stand in faith till death or till the Lords coming. Hence let us not hurry God and if it be God willing let it be done or else be happy the way it is because God wants you to be trained in some way to handle a tough situation ahead. I happened to meet a rape victim the first thing she told me was I have not wronged anyone or my parents have and why is this fate for me. You cannot retrieve the incident but you can, over time erase the memory with God's help and also you could be able to sound the warning bells in young teenage girls and counsel them from getting into a similar plight or you could help another victim to overcome the same problem. We can be positive in all matters good or bad. Many years back when I was a plus two student residing in the hostel campus I used to come home most of the weekends which was a four hours journey and Monday mornings I used to get back to college. One fine day by Gods grace I didn't hear the alarm ring, overslept and when I got up it was just 15min left for the train to depart. I rushed to railway station and managed to see the train slowly moving away. I was really worried I could get into trouble for missing two exams that day and finally managed to take a bus from the bus station. The bus was over crowded and I was cursing within my heart of why I did not hear the alarm and why I had to miss the train. After a long and tedious journey I managed to reach my college and also gave the two exams and then I heard the tragic accident of the train that I was supposed to be in. The train derailed into one of the deepest lakes and many people perished in that tragedy. I was thinking what a narrow escape and God knew exactly what was going to happen. Many times we miss flights, important meetings, marriages get postponed or cancelled, fail exams, fall sick, get maimed, and lose loved ones. We should not be dismayed if we are a true believer, for everything that happens there is a good purpose. Our impatience should not lead us to tragedies. If you have a genuine prayer request keep knocking, persistently our living God cannot shut his ears to a righteous man cry.

1Pe 2:20: For what glory is it, if, when ye sin, and are buffeted for it, ye shall take it patiently? but if, when ye do well, and suffer for it, ye shall take it patiently, this is acceptable with God.

1Pe 2:21: For hereunto were ye called: because Christ also suffered for you, leaving you an example, that ye should follow his steps:

Jas 1:3: Knowing that the proving of your faith worketh patience.

Jas 1:4: And let patience have *its* perfect work, that ye may be perfect and entire, lacking in nothing.

95

Over-anxious

People are anxious about their jobs, future, projects, finance, children's education, security, health and finally old age. In young age you worry for exams, adulthood, your partner and as you get older reasons to worry rise up. In short, the longer the life, reasons to worry expands in quantity. Our God tells us not to fret or worry over anything and questions us if we can change a grey hair to black? Even if the watchman is alert unless God chooses to protect us, we are not protected. The revelation from the Bible has made an indelible impact on my life. I first came to know Jesus from a Catholic school. During my undergraduate days, I used to be a temple visitor reading on Vedas and Koran. I was fascinated by the peaceful nature of Buddism and was praying to *the unknown God* to show me the right path.

One day, by a miracle, I was convinced that the Bible followed in its true sense is the right path. But still I never felt the closeness to God. Once I received the adult Baptism, I started knowing and feeling the closeness of God personally, then I realized one thing the old me used to be anxious over many matters but the new me takes one day at a time with no worry over anything bad or good and was instilled with inner peace.

Great trials and misfortunes can come your way, but if you are a true child of God nothing can shake you. You'll smile and shall take all worries in prayer to the Lord. I have seen the end of these trials to be the greatest blessings in my life. So a Godly child is given great peace, courage and encouragement by God to pass through all the trials, which is placed in a believer's life with peace. I can guarantee you that I have felt it only after being a true born again and this wisdom has come from the Lord.

Php 4:6: In nothing be anxious; but in everything by prayer and supplication with thanksgiving let your requests be made known unto God.

2Ti 1:7: For God gave us not a spirit of fearfulness; but of power and love and discipline.

96

Do Not Provoke Others

Never ever insult or tease God's children and never criticize on the work they do. Many harm God's children in many ways like beating them, spreading rumours about them or doing witch craft against them. Hostilities amongst religions grow out of sins. Provoking another religion publicly is wrong. If you don't like their ideals you need not follow them but don't criticize. I don't like idol worship, I don't do it but if someone does it, I never interfere or provoke them.

1Sa 24:6: And he said unto his men, The LORD forbid that I should do this thing unto my master, the LORD'S anointed, to stretch forth mine hand against him, seeing he *is* the anointed of the LORD. Hence if you provoke someone contrary to Biblical commandments and call yourself a martyr you are a liar.

Do not disrespect other people's religious beliefs. Many years back I used to wear the sandalwood tilak regularly on my forehead after visiting a temple. On one such visit as usual I was wearing the tilak, one of my friend who was then a born again commended 'hey why are you wearing a devils symbol on your forehead', I got so offended and vowed to myself that I will never have any respect for his God and thought in my mind what an uncouth religion to follow. But God had different plans for me, he forgave me and made me his. Never ever provoke or jest at another man's beliefs and ideas because you might be the very stumbling block for your brother, preventing him from loving your God. Another incident I vividly remember that when I was a junior lecturer in a college and the final year practical examinations were going on, me and one of my collegue were put on exam duty. My companion on exam duty was a staunch Hindu. The external examiner was a born again Christian, after the completion of every exam we used to have lunch together. On one such day the examiner was telling about the tragic story of her daughter who was suffering from a muscle atrophy disorder. After hearing the whole story my other colleague said "don't worry mam I will pray for your daughter" instantly the examiner retorted that she didn't need her prayer as it is offered to idols. The way she replied left us all in an uneasy situation and my colleague felt very insulted to the extent that she refused to talk to her after that. Lacking Diplomacy is a sin and is a sister to hypocrisy.

Pro 11:9: An hypocrite with *his* mouth destroyeth his neighbour: but through knowledge shall the just be delivered.

97

Lack of Hospitality

If you truly are a child of God you should receive guest with enthusiasm and offer good hospitality. Every Christian home should be open to guests and their needs. People should feel comfortable at your house and should feel like visiting you next time. Many times unknowingly a working class woman tired out of routine jobs hate visitors. But remember one thing; any visitor to your house is like Jesus at your house so treat them like Jesus. The present generation is not accommodative to guest, they hate to give up their space and room for any one. The children grumble when visitors come and the woman of the house curse in their hearts. I remember my mother at this point with gratitude, she was not a born again but the hospitality she extended to guest with prior notice or unexpected visitors was amazing. She always had a supply of food and goodies to pack back for visitors readily at hand. She had exemplary cooking skills and people liked to come and visit her and spend days with her to relax from their hectic schedules. Even after she passed away people used to remind me of her great hospitality. I feel ashamed that I didn't inherit it from my mother completely the way she did it.

1Pe 4:9: using hospitality one to another without murmuring.

Joh 13:20: "Verily, verily, I say unto you, He that receiveth whomsoever I send receiveth me; and he that receiveth me receiveth him that sent me."

Luk 9:48: And said unto them, "Whosoever shall receive this child in my name receiveth me: and whosoever shall receive me receiveth him that sent me: for he that is least among you all, the same shall be great."

Mat 10:40: "He that receiveth you receiveth me, and he that receiveth me receiveth him that sent me."

Mat 10:41: "He that receiveth a prophet in the name of a prophet shall receive a prophet's reward; and he that receiveth a righteous man in the name of a righteous man shall receive a righteous man's reward."

Mat 10:42: "And whosoever shall give to drink unto one of these little ones a cup of cold *water* only in the name of a disciple, verily I say unto you, he shall in no wise lose his reward."

98

Love for Gifts

Never expect anyone to lavish you with gifts for favours you have done. Never expect a favour back for doing another favour. Never think it is right that your juniors need to give gifts for favours they receive from you. Never take gifts from people who are manipulative, forcing you to judge in their favour.

Never compromise on principles by accepting gifts. The safest thing to do is not to accept any gift when you are in an authoritative position, a position that demands your impartial opinion on significant matters of the country, institution or society. But instead think on how much you can give in terms of your time, energy, money and knowledge whenever essential. Giving always gives you joy, peace and satisfaction.

I am narrating an incidence from my life. My routine is to work in a dental institution from 8.30 am to 3.30 pm followed by clinical practice in my clinic from 4.30 pm to 7.30 pm. Some days are really hectic, this was one such day. In college our final year practical exams were about to begin in few days and in clinic many patients were waiting. I was busy working on a patient then my assistant informed me that someone is waiting in the lobby without an appointment but seeks to see me urgently on some important matter. After completing my patient work & before starting on the next appointment I walked outside to see a mother of my student who was going to give practical exams soon. She was standing there smiling with a big gift. The Holy Spirit immediately reminded me the verse below and by Gods grace I refused to accept the same. A few days later the exams got over and that very student performed very badly in the practicals and failed the exams. I was glad that I have a heavenly father to guide me in all matters. If I had accepted it, that very lady could have said that after taking the gift I failed her son and if I had taken the gift though his performance was bad, my mind would be at unrest to fail him because the gift would stand in the way. These situations are called, between the devil and deep sea.

Exo 23:8: And thou shalt take no gift: for the gift blindeth the wise, and perverteth the words of the righteous.

Abraham refuses gift for saving:

Gen 14:23: That I will not *take* from a thread even to a shoelatchet, and that I will not take any thing that *is* thine, lest thou shouldest say, I have made Abram rich:

Gen 15:6: And he believed in the LORD; and he counted it to him for righteousness.

99

Miser

He is a person who hoards wealth and spends as little money as possible. There are two extremes to miserliness. Some of them spent for themselves but even if they have to waste food or throw it away they refuse to give it to others this happens with their ward robes too. Dresses keep accumulating in the cupboard which they are not using until the silver fishes feed on them. The other category will be stringent in buying food and clothes for themselves and sit in the dark without lights, so that they can save money on buying vegetables, food and electricity. I once encountered a person who eats only once a day, Wipes instead of taking bath so water charges can be saved on, rides a cycle to workplace, reuses the three shirts and trousers for a week, and had no friends for the fear of spending on them. What a way to live? The life God gave you is to spend for your personal needs. From my personal experience the more I gave, the double I got from God. Love this life and use your money and talents for the right cause. Here is what the Bible tells:

Pro 11:25: The liberal soul shall be made fat: and he that watereth shall be watered also himself.

Pro 11:26: He that withholdeth corn, the people shall curse him: but blessing *shall be* upon the head of him that selleth *it.*

Mar 12:44: "For all *they* did cast in of their abundance; but she of her want did cast in all that she had, *even* all her living".

Pro 22:9: He that hath a bountiful eye shall be blessed; for he giveth of his bread to the poor.

Pro 22:22: Rob not the poor, because he *is* poor: neither oppress the afflicted in the gate:

Pro 22:23: For the LORD will plead their cause, and spoil the soul of those that spoiled them.

100

Wanting to Know the Future

The unpredictability of the future lures people to seek to know about it somehow. For the sake of knowing the future they spend a lot of money on astrology, horoscope and so on. God expects men to take each day at a time and depend solely on God for the entire life. Many times God reveals the future and shows visions and dreams to his children for spiritual growth or as a warning. Bible repeatedly condemns people who are soothsayers, false prophets and people involved in witch craft. The Bible calls them the children of darkness. Hence, money spent to know the future by visiting astrologers, soothsayers, sorcerers, evil magicians and so called prophets are forms of sin equaling to idol worship and the punishments in the Bible for such is everlasting fire.

Unknown things are better left unknown. Never go to astrologers or fortune tellers nor show interest in the zodiac signs to know your future for a week, year or life time. Bible speaks of the great evil that can befall us while tackling the unknown or trying to counter-cross God. From the words of Jesus it's clear that all things are decided by the supreme God alone and no man can know anything of future until God chooses to reveal to that person for the admonition and preparation of mankind. Revelation was such a chapter for believers, not to lose faith and to have hope for eternal life. God only reveals matters when it can sustain souls till the end in order to encourage his children to strengthen their faith. Astrologers work like scientists; they have calculated assumptions of common scientific-based evidence over a long period of time which is recorded and hence they categorize individuals or events to precedence. A person born on this day is equated to great personalities born on that specific time. Need not be correct and every man is designed and God knows till his death what's going to happen to him. The only factor God does not control is one's thoughts. God leaves it to him to select the good or evil.

But he does give warnings for your choices as when Israelites asked for a king it displeased God, not because God's power was taken away but because he felt sorry for the future generations coming under a king. God tells them your children will be slaves you will lose freedom, all your land will be the king's, your wives will be taken away and all this happened. Yet the Israelites where so adamant that they wanted a king and God let them have their desire. So the moral of the story is don't ask God for things, just pray to God and let His holy will be done in your life. Lots of examples (Balaam and Jonah) who chose their way and had trouble are recorded in the Bible for our own good. We need to keep them in our minds and apply the moral of each Biblical story to our own lives.

Hence, do not worry for tomorrow or show eagerness to know of it. Only God can tell what's going to happen the very next second in your life, neither man nor the very devils nor the angels in heaven knows unless revealed by the mighty God himself. God hates people who look for signs and miracles. God loves people who ask and humbly accepts Gods decisions in their lives. Total submission to God in all aspects is required.

My greatest mistake:

Before knowing the true God, I was really interested in not only this life and death but the past life too. My father also believes in this and showed keen interest in these matters. So we embarked on our journey to a remote village in southern India where with a mere thumb impression they say who you are? what your name is? what your future profession? what are your fate and curses? And of course what you were in your last birth? Keen on knowing all this we spent thousands of money. The entire data comes in an old leaf written with quilt and ink. With your thumb impression they start reading out one by one from a few selected leaflets until your name, your fathers and mothers name are correct then they confirm it is your life. My life was read out, the curses were, that in my last birth I was a dignitary, I had been cruel to men and so this birth if I don't make amendments for the same I will remain unmarried. My father agreed to the giving, it was some silver wares to few temples. Luckily when I saw that huge amount was involved I adamantly told my dad I rather stay unmarried and after some discussions on the practicality aspects, we returned from that place to our home town. Besides these it is a culture in our families to write the horoscope of the new born child with the star sign and the time the child was born. My mother had already got my life documented. But once I became a born again and when I was praying for the right partner in my life I was reminded by God to get these documents out of my life and I permanently destroyed them. Today without any sacrifices to temple I am happily married in Christ. Hence, when you are praying for an important matter of your life, keep your mind focused and listen to the still voice of God for your blessings.

Isa 47:12: Stand now with thine enchantments, and with the multitude of thy sorceries, wherein thou hast laboured from thy youth; if so be thou shalt be able to profit, if so be thou mayest prevail.

Isa 47:13: Thou art wearied in the multitude of thy counsels. Let now the astrologers, the stargazers, the monthly prognosticators, stand up, and save thee from *these things* that shall come upon thee.

101

Lack of Testimony

One of the most significant criteria for ultimate Christian life is your testimony amongst people around you and God. We have covered the entire list of sins and the preceding chapters elaborates on how a good Christian should be. Your neighbors', colleagues and family should be able to see Christ in you and in all what you do. They should feel like wanting to know more about you and what is the secret behind the success and happiness in your life? The Bible says it all

1Pe 2:12: having your behavior seemly among the Gentiles; that, wherein they speak against you as evil-doers, they may by your good works, which they behold, glorify God in the day of visitation.

Php 2:15: that ye may become blameless and harmless, children of God without blemish in the midst of a crooked and perverse generation, among whom ye are seen as lights in the world.

Few years back, I happened to visit Tokyo dental university and was staying at Ochanamizu. I found an assembly close to this place. One Sunday I met Brother Joel from U.S. I have previously met many citizens from U.S of different backgrounds but this Brother was full of Godliness and talked the right words. After meeting him talking to him and hearing his messages I changed all the wrong notions I had of U.S. Until I met him I thought that U.S was a nation not holding Godly values in its true sense, more modern in outlook and luke warm in faith. Imagine a single good believer can stand for a nation. What a testimony?

SECTION 4
CONCLUSION

A Good Christian

A Christian is a person who follows Christ in all aspects. He has accepted Jesus Christ as his saviour, is committed to Christ by baptism and obeys the commandments set forth by God, leads this life as per the will of God and his life is a testimony to God and men. He projects Christ in his behaviour by his good work, good speech and good guidance.

1Jn 5:10: He that believeth on the Son of God hath the witness in him: he that believeth not God hath made him a liar; because he hath not believed in the witness that God hath borne concerning his Son.

1Jn 5:11: And the witness is this, that God gave unto us eternal life, and this life is in his Son.

1Jn 5:12: He that hath the Son hath the life; he that hath not the Son of God hath not the life.

OF GOOD WORK:

Fasting and praying supporting a matter.

Helping with finance or physical help.

Helping others when in need.

Giving alms.

Supporting the weak.

Hospitality.

Standing for righteousness.

Long suffering.

Patience.

Forgiveness.

Faithful man.

Prayerful life---What are the things we ought to pray for?

- Daily provisions of God.
- Your thoughts to be God's will and your prayer should be according to the will of God.
- Your family and friends.
- Your neighbourhood.
- Your foes and enemies, if any.
- Your job and all things you do that day, to know if it's God's will.
- Your country, world and the leaders,
- For Jerusalem and its peace,
- For God's holy day to worship in spirit and truth.
- For your soul and the coming of the Lord,
- For people who asked your prayer support.
- For the drug addicts, sinners jailed ones, prostitutes and matters the Holy Spirit guides you to pray for.
- Your children and husband.

The first essential quality any believer should possess is prayer life. A person can neither give peace of mind to another Brother nor solve all his marital or his financial problems, but can ask in prayer to the mighty God to solve all problems for this friend of him as if it is his own problem. The model of prayer Jesus taught is to pray early in the morning and before going to bed. To steadfastly pray, unceasingly pray, believing and pray, pray with thanksgiving, pray with a peaceful mind with no enmity to any one.

Do not pray for publicity stunts, do not pray for money, and do not pray with vain repetitions. Prayer should come from your heart. Pray earnestly with a clean heart. This is the greatest help you can do for your friends as good work, not only for friends but for all whom you are inspired to pray for. (*Joh 17:15*) Some good works are seen by others as good deeds but prayer is not seen by others yet you can perceive the change in the other person's life.

A believer's greatest strength is prayer life. A Christian who spends his time with God can achieve all success in this life. He is protected in mind and body. He is at peace during trials and is happy at all times. Pray in time of confusion, in time of unease and unrest of mind, pray when you doubt, pray when you are tensed and anxious, pray when you tend to move away from God, pray for others and their needs, pray for your sins to be forgiven, pray for major decisions in life. When all matters are kept in prayer, the will of God manifests.

Every Brother or Sister in Christ should love the human race regardless of caste and creed and should treat everyone like how he or she wishes to be treated. Anyone who goes out of the way to help neighbors in need will be definitely rewarded by the heavenly father. *Mat 7:12* - "Therefore all things whatsoever ye would that men should do to you, do ye even so to them: for this is the law and the prophets."

Prayers can be many types one such prayer is an earnest short time prayer, when you remember a matter and then forget it for a long time and then again you pray, this is inconsistent prayer. The second type is consistent earnest prayer, this is extremely difficult to do unless you are a real committed Christian the third type is fasting and praying supporting a matter (*Est 4:16*) The fourth type is an interceding prayer, very useful to change bad situations that are going to take place. *Deu 9:25* Thus I fell down before the LORD forty days and forty nights, as I fell down *at the first;* because the LORD had said he would destroy you.

How to Pray:

Psa 143:8: Cause me to hear thy loving kindness in the morning; for in thee do I trust: cause me to know the way wherein I should walk; for I lift up my soul unto thee.

Mat 21:22: "And all things, whatsoever ye shall ask in prayer, believing, ye shall receive."

Mar 1:35: And in the morning, rising up a great while before day, he went out, and departed into a solitary place, and there prayed.

Col 4:2: Continue stedfastly in prayer, watching therein with thanksgiving;

Col 4:3: withal praying for us also, that God may open unto us a door for the word, to speak the mystery of Christ, for which I am also in bonds;

1Ti 2:1: I exhort therefore, first of all, that supplications, prayers, intercessions, thanksgivings, be made for all men;

1Ti 2:2: for kings and all that are in high place; that we may lead a tranquil and quiet life in all godliness and gravity.

1Ti 2:8: I desire therefore that the men pray in every place, lifting up holy hands, without wrath and disputing.

Mat 6:6: "But thou, when thou prayest, enter into thy closet, and when thou hast shut thy door, pray to thy Father which is in secret; and thy Father which seeth in secret shall reward thee openly."

Mat 6:7: "But when ye pray, use not vain repetitions, as the heathen *do:* for they think that they shall be heard for their much speaking."

Psa 122:6: Pray for the peace of Jerusalem: they shall prosper that love thee.

Helping:

The second most essential quality a Christian should possess is love, from which generates all other good qualities. As said in Corinthians, love is longsuffering, patient, and gentle and it does not hurt others, it accepts others. A Christian without love is like a Christian with no Christ in him.

Kindness and mercy are manifestations of love. Bible refers to love as a minimum standard to enter eternal life.

Help in any form that can bring relief to another brother is of Godly nature. If a Brother is extremely poor, you need to help him with finance or if an old widow needs an errand to be done urgently you should offer your help.

Luk 11:41: "But rather give alms of such things as ye have; and, behold, all things are clean unto you."

Helping for good things in Christ is becoming scarce as everyone is busy with their own workloads and financial security. Always possess a kind heart to help; going that extra mile for the other person, benefits you because heavenly father has promised to repay you in some way.

Pro 11:25: The liberal soul shall be made fat: and he that watereth shall be watered also himself.

Jas 2:15: If a brother or sister be naked and in lack of daily food,

Jas 2:16: and one of you say unto them, Go in peace, be ye warmed and filled; and yet ye give them not the things needful to the body; what doth it profit?

Helping is a vast terminology it includes the fact that you as a person brings joy, courage, and love into another person's life. This can be in many ways; a financial help to a school student, physical help to an old person with no one, standing by someone and talking for him when the other is in trouble and sometimes your mere physical presence can lighten another person's life.

Act 20:35: I have shewed you all things, how that so labouring ye ought to support the weak, and to remember the words of the Lord Jesus, how he said, "It is more blessed to give than to receive."

Good hospitality, patient hearing and sometimes understanding the underlying cause of a depressed or angry Brother's reaction can enable you to tackle him well with kind words that can be a balm to his wounded heart. This might even help the depressed brother to tide over the bad time he is going through. Forgive all and do not hold grudge on anyone. Any visitor to your house should be treated with respect, love and kindness considering him as Christ himself.

Heb 13:2: Forget not to show love unto strangers: for thereby some have entertained angels unawares.

1Pe 4:8: above all things being fervent in your love among yourselves; for love covereth a multitude of sins:

A person who can forgive others and treat them with love always has more chance of gaining a lost Brother. The story of the Good

Samaritan clearly shows that people considered as pious need not help people. A Levi and priest passed by without helping finally it was the Samaritan, a person not much favored by Jews, was the one who helped the wounded man. (Luk 10:33-34)

Pro 11:30: The fruit of the righteous *is* a tree of life; and he that winneth souls *is* wise.

Stand for righteousness:

When you are a public figure, world leader or a decision maker always ask this question; Is my God pleased with my decision? Am I making it for the glory of God? Am I hurting Gods principles or sentiments in any way? Am I harming Gods people in any way?, if you get a negative answer from God BEWARE you are in line of Balaam and you will be soon gone and your position is going to be taken away from you, dishonor is in store for you.

Pro 3:27: Withhold not good from them to whom it is due, when it is in the power of thine hand to do *it*.

Your unrighteous decision to get more vote banks will collapse if the Lord is not for it. On the contrary if your decision is God favoring and not men pleasing you are safe because though tens of thousands of people stand against you, your mighty God will honour you and will hold the post for you, though great resistance can occur in terms of verbal slander from men around you, God will uphold you daily and the mighty God will himself come down to deliver you.

Est 4:13: Then Mordecai commanded to answer Esther, Think not with thyself that thou shalt escape in the king's house, more than all the Jews.

Pro 20:6: Most men will proclaim everyone his own goodness: but a faithful man who can find?

Pro 20:7: The just *man* walketh in his integrity: his children *are* blessed after him.

Pro 28:20: A faithful man shall abound with blessings: but he that maketh haste to be rich shall not be innocent.

Long suffering/Patience/Forgiveness:

In day to day life people are extremely impatient, the rich think money can buy them anything, the mediocre think that using influence can get them what they want and the poor think that those tough muscular men and the rich and influential only survive. They achieve what they want without patiently seeking Gods council on what is good.

1Pe 2:20: For what glory is it, if, when ye sin, and are buffeted *for it*, ye shall take it patiently? but if, when ye do well, and suffer *for it*, ye shall take it patiently, this is acceptable with God.

Jas 1:4: And let patience have *its* perfect work, that ye may be perfect and entire, lacking in nothing.

A good person in Christ need to be patient long suffering and forgiving.

Mat 6:14: "For if ye forgive men their trespasses, your heavenly Father will also forgive you:"

Mat 6:15: "But if ye forgive not men their trespasses, neither will your Father forgive your trespasses."

It's always best to keep all decisions in prayer first before making a hasty decision. God knows the best about you and the ways ahead of you. To prolong any relationship in this world with peace and love you need to possess these three essential qualities.

Mat 12:35: "A good man out of the good treasure of the heart bringeth forth good things: and an evil man out of the evil treasure bringeth forth evil things."

Good works by good speech:

A person who can turn off anger by a pleasant reply is a child of God. How a believer speaks matters a lot. Good speech includes.

Speaking truth.

A wise speech that can correct a person but not hurt them.

Stern to correct but with love.

Blessings should proceed from a good soul not curses.

A soft reply.

A kind answer.

Always able to answer with positiveness.

Words of encouragement, words of consolation, words of good advice, words aptly spoken in each situation are all the grace of God to any person.

If your tongue gets you in trouble for lying, boasting, backbiting and spreading false rumours and you claim that you are believer then God says you are not his child. Harsh words and rude manners are hurting. A soft answer is always preferred than a harsh reply. Every Christian who lives by the biblical principles ought to answer pleasantly and be positive in his/her thinking. All good works come from good heart and good thoughts. Only a person guided by the Holy Spirit can be good. For a man to be alive needs air, water and food. For a man's soul to live he needs Jesus, Holy Spirit and prayer. Without Jesus no man can reach God. You need the breath of God for your soul, Holy Spirit for guiding you in day to day life as water and prayer to make you healthy in body, mind and soul. Speech is an output of your inner self. Every word that proceeds from your mouth can give an intelligent person a clue to what type of an individual you are. Remember to talk to each person as per their age and give elders due respect while making your points for correction clear.

1Ti 5:1: Rebuke not an elder, but exhort him as a father; the younger men as brethren:

1Ti 5:2: the elder women as mothers; the younger as sisters, in all purity.

Quietness is a great asset it helps us to observe and analyze people. Communication is a God given gift and people who possess it are peacemakers and God loves them. An intelligent answer can prevent lot of wrath and hatred.

Heb 13:16: But to do good and to communicate forget not: for with such sacrifices God is well pleased.

Col 4:6: Let your speech be always with grace, seasoned with salt, that ye may know how ye ought to answer each one.

Jas 3:17: But the wisdom that is from above is first pure, then peaceable, gentle, easy to be entreated, full of mercy and Godly.

Heb 12:14: Follow after peace with all men, and the sanctification without which no man shall see the Lord:

Pro 3:30: Strive not with a man without cause, if he have done thee no harm.

Eph 4:32: and be ye kind one to another, tenderhearted, forgiving each other, even as God also in Christ forgave you.

Good guidance:

A good Christian is able to guide his friend or neighbors in the right direction. His council consoles and comforts his friend. He stands by them in trouble and he is of an understanding heart. He admonishes his friend and warns him of dangers. He is not a hypocrite. He talks the truth to his friend. Many times people come to you for guidance, the foremost thing that should cross your mind is what is the matter he has come for guidance? Is it for a good cause? Is it for peaceful matter? Is it for a righteous cause?, if so then you may give guidance and if not you need to intelligently talk him out of the evil he is planning to do. Many times we refuse to give the right advice for the fear of being hated or criticized but a righteous man after hearing a bad plot, not only strongly opposes it but also keeps the matter in prayer asking God to change this persons mind regarding the evil he is plotting. This is when a good Christian intercedes by the power of his prayer and is able to stop an impending disaster.

Pro 28:10: Whoso causeth the righteous to go astray in an evil way, he shall fall himself into his own pit: but the upright shall have good *things* in possession.

Pro 16:20: He that handleth a matter wisely shall find good: and whoso trusteth in the LORD, happy *is* he.

Common matters that come for counseling are marital issues, property fights between siblings, money disputes and ego clashes.

Jesus gives a beautiful example of tax collection; if it's a Government law regarding money matters, Jesus asked his disciples to give it but if it was an order as the one prophet Daniel faced then oppose it with faith and peace in God.

Mat 17:25: He saith, Yes. And when he was come into the house, Jesus prevented him, saying, "What thinkest thou, Simon? of whom do the kings of the earth take custom or tribute? of their own children, or of strangers?"

Mat 17:26: Peter saith unto him, Of strangers. Jesus saith unto him, "Then are the children free".

Mat 17:27: "Notwithstanding, lest we should offend them, go thou to the sea, and cast an hook, and take up the fish that first cometh up; and when thou hast opened his mouth, thou shalt find a piece of money: that take, and give unto them for me and thee".

If it's a property issue Bible clearly states to take it to the elders and the wise holy people and abide by their final decision and do not take it to court.

1Co 6:1: Dare any of you, having a matter against his neighbor, go to law before the unrighteous, and not before the saints?

1Co 6:2: Or know ye not that the saints shall judge the world? and if the world is judged by you, are ye unworthy to judge the smallest matters?

1Co 6:3: Know ye not that we shall judge angels? how much more, things that pertain to this life?

Third essential quality for every Christian is humility:

Every Christian should be humble enough to accept the fact that all what he possess is not by his own credit but by the grace of God. Whatever you do, how much effort you put in your work or studies, is ultimately Gods grace that sees you through. So every Christian should have this in mind that unless God blesses you, you cannot achieve anything. But the moment you start claiming that all what you have is your effort and don't give glory to God then you will start declining in spirituality.

Humble Christians give all glory to God and are well favoured by colleagues and every one respects them.

Mat 20:27: "And whosoever will be chief among you, let him be your servant":

Mat 20:28: "Even as the Son of man came not to be ministered unto, but to minister, and to give his life a ransom for many."

The believer stands out from others in a crowd cause of his meekness, peaceful nature, wise speech, truthfulness, dependability, righteousness, standing for justice, making his point clear without arguments, understanding, longsuffering, helpful, respectful, giving, sharing, caring, hospitality, prayerful, standing for God, not compromising on principles, loving, dutiful, cheerful, encouraging, prompt, disciplined and above all positive thinking in all aspect of life with strong faith in God's guidance.

The above-mentioned fruitful Christian is a rare entity in this world. His mannerisms are pleasant and he is God's child. Such a child's speech is filled with testimony of God, love, wise words, good advice, which will turn others wrath. They are peacemakers and as Bible tells surely they inherit the eternal kingdom. Every child of God is meant to be an encouragement, comfort and support for someone every day. A believer through his works should have a good testimony with man and God. Good testimony indicates righteous living, good name, honour, and respect from all including the devil. Even the devil knows the righteous man. As child of God even if you commit sins you can cry with true repentance to God and he is kind and merciful enough to forgive you.

Commandments for Elders/Pastors/Deacons/Priests/Prophets:

These days people take God's work for granted. Any person maimed or diseased is separated for God's work because they don't have any other job to do. God specifically demands that when you separate things for him, they should be unblemished. A worker for God has the strictest criteria set out by God in the Bible. Hence, any person intending to be a worker for God needs to closely follow the Bible and evaluate himself if he is worthy for God's work. If you critically evaluate yourself, you will not have the heavy hand of God falling on you.

In the present days, every man claims to be a pastor, elder or deacon without looking into the word of God. Hence the notion that the only responsibility is to just convert souls is a false doctrine. If any person has nagged someone to be a Christian and bribed him to do so, taking money for praying, has earned his livelihood by miracles, has had multiple marriages, committed adultery, given money on usury, lived a lavish lifestyle by the donations meant for the poor, has a broken family with children not obedient to him, is a drunkard, has lustful thoughts, does not keep quiet time, does not seek the face of God, does not dress according to the will of God, I recommend that they read the Bible thoroughly, and if they are not qualified as per the Bible, then graciously step out of the position, or else God is going to strip them and condemn them forever. Every elder/person holding a reputable position leading the rest of flock should adhere to all the qualities mentioned below or you are trying God. It could be more forgivable if you walked as you want and not hold on to Godly positions.

Be examples to others,

Full of good work,

Without reproach,

The husband of one wife,

Temperate,

Sober-minded,

Orderly,

Given to hospitality,

Apt to teach,

No brawler,

No striker,

Gentle,

Not contentious,

No lover of money,

One that rules well his own house, having his children in subjection with all gravity,

Good testimony with man and God,

Grave,

Not double-tongued,

Not given to much wine,

Not greedy of filthy lucre,

Holding the mystery of the faith in a pure conscience,

Not self-willed,

Just,

Holy,

Not soon angry,

Exhort in the sound doctrine,

Able convict the gainsayers,

Temperate,

Sound in faith,

Having love and patience.

Elder:

1Pe 5:3: neither as lording it over the charge allotted to you, but making yourselves ensamples to the flock.

1Ti 5:17: Let the elders that rule well be counted worthy of double honor, especially those who labor in the word and in teaching.

1Ti 5:19: Against an elder receive not an accusation, except at *the mouth of* two or three witnesses.

1Ti 5:20: Them that sin reprove in the sight of all that the rest also may be in fear.

Bishops:

1Ti 3:1: Faithful is the saying, If a man seeketh the office of a bishop, he desireth a good work.

1Ti 3:2: The bishop therefore must be without reproach, the husband of one wife, temperate, sober-minded, orderly, given to hospitality, apt to teach;

1Ti 3:3: no brawler, no striker; but gentle, not contentious, no lover of money;

1Ti 3:4: one that ruleth well his own house, having *his* children in subjection with all gravity;

1Ti 3:5: (but if a man knoweth not how to rule his own house, how shall he take care of the church of God?)

1Ti 3:6: not a novice, lest being puffed up he fall into the condemnation of the devil.

1Ti 3:7: Moreover he must have good testimony from them that are without; lest he fall into reproach and the snare of the devil.

Tit 1:6: if any man is blameless, the husband of one wife, having children that believe, who are not accused of riot or unruly.

Tit 1:7: For the bishop must be blameless, as God's steward; not self-willed, not soon angry, no brawler, no striker, not greedy of filthy lucre;

Tit 1:8: but given to hospitality, a lover of good, sober-minded, just, holy, self-controlled;

Tit 1:9: holding to the faithful word which is according to the teaching, that he may be able to exhort in the sound doctrine, and to convict the gainsayers.

Deacons:

1Ti 3:8: Deacons in like manner *must be* grave, not double-tongued, not given to much wine, not greedy of filthy lucre;

1Ti 3:9: holding the mystery of the faith in a pure conscience.

1Ti 3:10: And let these also first be proved; then let them serve as deacons, if they be blameless.

1Ti 3:12: Let deacons be husbands of one wife, ruling *their* children and their own houses well.

1Ti 3:13: For they that have served well as deacons gain to themselves a good standing, and great boldness in the faith which is in Christ Jesus.

Pastors:

Jer 23:1: Woe be unto the pastors that destroy and scatter the sheep of my pasture! saith the LORD.

Jer 23:2: Therefore thus saith the LORD God of Israel against the pastors that feed my people; Ye have scattered my flock, and driven them away, and have not visited them: behold, I will visit upon you the evil of your doings, saith the LORD.

Mat 23:16: Woe unto you, *ye* blind guides, which say, Whosoever shall swear by the temple, it is nothing; but whosoever shall swear by the gold of the temple, he is a debtor!

Prophets:

2Pe 1:21: For no prophecy ever came by the will of man: but men spake from God, being moved by the Holy Spirit.

2Pe 2:1: But there arose false prophets also among the people, as among you also there shall be false teachers, who shall privily bring in destructive heresies, denying even the Master that bought them, bringing upon themselves swift destruction.

2Pe 2:2: And many shall follow their lascivious doings; by reason of whom the way of the truth shall be evil spoken of.

Command to workers of God:

Evaluate yourselves and know if you have a mindset to be a child of God.

Today, we hear more prayer requests not centered on serving others, but for the construction of halls and assemblies. Why make a place of worship when believers are only few. If you need a worship place believe that God is able to provide for you through his children. Many times I have been reminded in my quiet time to immediately help a person. These people are not the one who regularly keep in touch with me. When you sit and pray, the Holy Spirit guides you to help others. This is called divine provision. But, when I am requested for donation, I generally give but always wonder if it is the will of God. In earlier days, elders never shared their poverty status or need of money with any one, they sat and prayed and God moved many a heart through various miracles. Today pastors' or elders' financial needs are announced and well known to all. Is this Godly? Personally this issue bothers me. When I have a deep desire for something I ask God in prayer and wait. Many days pass by I get no reply, I start fasting and then two things happen: either it gets done or I am assured to wait and if it is not God's will I stop the prayer request and the desire leaves me. To all God's children in the field of work and outside, God is our treasure and is able to provide what we wants provided it is also God's will.

What commandment did God give the pastors, preachers and disciples?

Mat 10:8: Heal the sick, cleanse the lepers, raise the dead, cast out devils: freely ye have received, freely give.

Mat 10:9: Provide neither gold, nor silver, nor brass in your purses,

Mat 10:10: Nor scrip for *your* journey, neither two coats, neither shoes, nor yet staves: for the workman is worthy of his meat.

Mat 10:13: And if the house be worthy, let your peace come upon it: but if it be not worthy, let your peace return to you.

Mat 10:14: And whosoever shall not receive you, nor hear your words, when ye depart out of that house or city, shake off the dust of your feet.

Mat 10:28: And fear not them which kill the body, but are not able to kill the soul: but rather fear him which is able to destroy both soul and body in hell.

From all the above verses there is no forceful collection of money in any way to build places of worship. None of the Old Testament (except Jerusalem Temple) and New Testament preachers or prophets did construction work. It was done by believers.

Conclusion

1Co 3:13: each man's work shall be made manifest: for the day shall declare it, because it is revealed in fire; and the fire itself shall prove each man's work of what sort it is.

Col 1:10: to walk worthily of the Lord unto all pleasing, bearing fruit in every good work, and increasing in the knowledge of God;

Php 4:8: Finally, brethren, whatsoever things are true, whatsoever things are honorable, whatsoever things are just, whatsoever things are pure, whatsoever things are lovely, whatsoever things are of good report; if there be any virtue, and if there be any praise, think on these things.

Ecc 12:13: Let us hear the conclusion of the whole matter: Fear God, and keep his commandments: for this *is* the whole *duty* of man.

Amen

Index